Artistic Inspiration - The Top 500 "In The Style Of" Ai Art Prompts

Michael Ferguson

Published by Michael Ferguson, 2023.

ARTISTIC INSPIRATION - THE TOP 500 "IN THE STYLE OF" AI ART PROMPTS

First edition. April 17, 2023.

ISBN: 979-8215140888

Written by Michael Ferguson.

Table of Contents

Welcome to "Artistic Inspiration - The Top 500 "In The Style Of" Ai Art Prompts! In this book, you'll discover a fascinating world where art and artificial intelligence intersect, unlocking new possibilities for your creativity.

One of the exciting features of this book is the use of prompts that include "In the style of" followed by the name of a renowned artist who has been trained on AI art generators datasets. These prompts are designed to inspire you and guide you in creating art that emulates the style of your favorite artists. For example, you may come across a prompt like "In the style of Piet Mondrian," which can inspire you to create a piece of abstract art using Mondrian's iconic geometric compositions and bold color palette.

However, it's important to note that AI-generated prompts are not foolproof and may not always produce the desired results. AI algorithms are trained on vast amounts of data, but they are not perfect and can sometimes produce outputs that may not perfectly match the style of the artist mentioned in the prompt. That's why it's essential to approach these prompts with an open mind and be willing to experiment and iterate to find the best combination of prompts that work for you.

Before You Start:

Before diving into the world of AI-generated art prompts, it's important to understand that not all prompts will work perfectly every time. It's normal to encounter some inconsistencies or deviations from the desired style, and that's okay. The key is to approach it as a creative journey and be open to experimentation.

To make the most of this book, we encourage you to test out different combinations of prompts, explore various artists and their styles, and even engineer your own unique styles by tweaking and modifying the prompts. Remember, the goal is not to simply replicate an artist's work, but to use the prompts as a starting point to ignite your own creativity and create your unique masterpieces.

Every name mentioned below can be used in a prompt for Ai art generation. Please make sure to use the "In the style of" prompt to get the best use. For example, "Draw a beautiful portrait of a woman with feline traits in the style of Dan Mumford" Which would create a 2d illustration/digital painting close to the style of Dan Mumford if not spot on. I personally use Dan Mumford quite often and find this prompt creates exciting art.

So, get ready to embark on an exciting artistic adventure and let the power of AI inspire and elevate your art to new heights! Remember, the possibilities are endless, and with experimentation and creativity, you can unlock the full potential of "Artistic Inspiration." Happy creating!

Thomas Kinkade: Painter - Thomas Kinkade was an American painter known for his idyllic and picturesque landscapes, often featuring cozy cottages, peaceful gardens, and serene natural settings. He was a prolific artist whose works are characterized by their luminous and warm palette, inviting compositions, and nostalgic themes. Kinkade's paintings have been widely reproduced and collected, and he is often referred to as the "Painter of Light" for his skillful use of light and shadow in his artworks.

Vincent Van Gogh: Painter - Vincent Van Gogh was a Dutch post-impressionist painter known for his expressive and vibrant artworks, particularly his cityscapes and landscape paintings. His works are characterized by their bold brushwork, vivid colors, and emotional intensity. Van Gogh's paintings often depict ordinary scenes with a unique and subjective perspective, capturing the beauty and essence of the natural world in a distinctive style. Despite struggling with mental illness and facing numerous challenges during his lifetime, Van Gogh's artworks have become iconic and influential in the world of art.

Leonid Afremov: Painter - Leonid Afremov was a Russian-Israeli painter known for his unique and vibrant artworks that often depict cityscapes, landscapes, and rainy streets. His works are characterized by their bold use of color, impressionistic style, and evocative atmosphere. Afremov's paintings are instantly recognizable for their distinctive palette knife technique and the sense of emotion and mood they convey. His artworks have gained widespread popularity and are collected by art enthusiasts around the world.

Claude Monet: Painter - Claude Monet was a French impressionist painter known for his groundbreaking works in landscape art and portraiture. His paintings are characterized by their loose brushwork, vibrant colors, and emphasis on capturing the changing effects of light and atmosphere. Monet's innovative approach to painting, which focused on capturing the fleeting moments of nature, had a profound impact on the development of modern art. His iconic series of paintings, such as the Water Lilies and Haystacks, are considered masterpieces of impressionism.

Edward Hopper: Painter - Edward Hopper was an American painter known for his genre paintings and American realism style. His works often depict solitary figures in urban settings, capturing the sense of isolation and emptiness of modern life. Hopper's paintings are characterized by their stark compositions, moody lighting, and meticulous attention to detail. His works are often seen as reflections of the human condition and have been recognized for their psychological depth and emotional impact.

Norman Rockwell: Painter - Norman Rockwell was an American painter and illustrator known for his realistic and nostalgic depictions of American life. His works often depict everyday scenes, family moments, and small-town America, capturing the essence of American culture and values. Rockwell's paintings are characterized by their meticulous attention to detail, warm colors, and storytelling quality. His artworks have been widely reproduced and have become iconic representations of American life and values.

William-Adolphe Bouguereau: Painter - William-Adolphe Bouguereau was a French painter known for his mythological paintings and association with the Pont-Aven School. His works are characterized by their exquisite craftsmanship, idealized figures, and dreamlike quality. Bouguereau's paintings often depict mythological and allegorical themes, showcasing his skill in capturing the human form with precision and grace. His artworks have been highly regarded for their technical mastery and artistic beauty.

Albert Bierstadt: Painter - Albert Bierstadt was a German American painter known for his stunning landscapes of the American West. His works are characterized by their grand scale, majestic scenery, and meticulous attention to detail. Bierstadt's paintings often depict breathtaking vistas of mountains, forests, and lakes, capturing the awe-inspiring beauty of the American wilderness. He was known for his ability to capture the dramatic light and atmospheric effects of the landscapes he painted, creating a sense of awe and wonder in his viewers. Bierstadt's works were highly popular during his time and continue to be admired for their majestic beauty and technical skill.

John Singer Sargent: Painter - John Singer Sargent was an American painter known for his portraits and landscape paintings. He was renowned for his exceptional skill in capturing the likeness and personality of his subjects, as well as his masterful use of light and color. Sargent's portraits are characterized by their elegance, sophistication, and attention to detail, and his landscape paintings often depict scenes from his travels around the world, showcasing his ability to capture the beauty of nature in different settings. His works are considered masterpieces of portrait and landscape painting and have earned him widespread acclaim and recognition.

Pierre-Auguste Renoir: Painter - Pierre-Auguste Renoir was a French painter known for his mythological paintings and landscape art. He was a leading figure in the Impressionist movement and known for his innovative use of color, light, and brushwork. Renoir's works are characterized by their lush and vibrant palette, soft and delicate brushwork, and celebration of everyday life. His mythological paintings often depict scenes from ancient mythology with a sense of beauty and sensuality, while his landscape art captures the charm and serenity of the natural world. Renoir's works are highly regarded for their beauty, charm, and technical skill.

Frida Kahlo: Painter - Frida Kahlo was a Mexican painter known for her surrealist and self-portrait paintings. She is considered one of the most important and influential artists of the 20th century, known for her deeply personal and introspective artworks that often depicted her physical and emotional pain, as well as her cultural heritage. Kahlo's works are characterized by their bold and vibrant colors, symbolic imagery, and powerful emotional expression. Her self-portraits are particularly notable, showcasing her unique style and perspective as a woman and artist. Kahlo's artworks have been recognized for their raw honesty, feminist themes, and profound impact on the art world.

John William Waterhouse: Painter - John William Waterhouse was a British painter known for his works influenced by the Pre-Raphaelite Brotherhood and his depictions of mythological and literary themes. His works are characterized by their rich colors, intricate details, and romanticized style. Waterhouse's paintings often depict mythological and allegorical scenes with a sense of mystery, beauty, and sensuality. He was known for his exceptional skill in capturing the human form and his ability to create a sense of enchantment in his artworks. Waterhouse's works have been highly regarded for their poetic and evocative quality, and he is considered one of the prominent figures of the Pre-Raphaelite movement.

Winslow Homer: Painter - Winslow Homer was an American painter known for his realist artworks, particularly his marine art and depictions of American life. He was known for his ability to capture the power and beauty of the sea in his paintings, as well as his insightful portrayals of everyday life in America. Homer's works are characterized by their meticulous attention to detail, bold compositions, and emotional intensity. His marine art often depicts the dramatic and tumultuous nature of the sea, while his genre paintings capture the simple yet profound moments of everyday life. Homer's artworks are highly regarded for their technical skill, emotional depth, and social commentary.

Walt Disney: Artist - Walt Disney was an American entrepreneur, animator, and filmmaker, known for his pioneering work in animation and entertainment industry. He co-founded The Walt Disney Company and was a pioneer in developing innovative techniques and technologies in animation, making it one of the most successful entertainment companies in history. Disney's artistic contributions revolutionized the animation industry and transformed the way stories are told through visual media. He was known for his creativity, imagination, and innovation, and his iconic characters such as Mickey Mouse and Donald Duck have become beloved symbols of popular culture. In addition to animation, Disney also made significant contributions to theme park design and concept art, creating immersive worlds that continue to captivate audiences around the globe. His artistic vision and entrepreneurial spirit have left an indelible mark on the entertainment industry and continue to inspire artists and storytellers to this day.

Thomas Moran: Painter - Thomas Moran was an American painter known for his exploratory landscape art, particularly his depictions of the American West. He was a prominent member of the Hudson River School, a group of landscape painters who focused on capturing the beauty of the American wilderness. Moran's works are characterized by their grandeur, majestic landscapes, and attention to detail. His paintings often depict scenes from the Rocky Mountains, Yellowstone National-al Park, and other natural wonders of the American West, showcasing his skill in capturing the awe-inspiring beauty of these landscapes. Moran's works have been highly regarded for their technical excellence, sense of adventure, and contributions to the preservation of America's natural treasures.

Phil Koch: Artist - Phil Koch is a contemporary American artist known for his unique style of landscape paintings. He is known for his "imaginative realism" approach, which combines elements of surrealism, symbolism, and fantasy to create dreamlike landscapes that evoke a sense of mystery, wonder, and emotional resonance. Koch's works are characterized by their rich and vibrant colors, detailed textures, and surreal imagery that often blend elements of the natural world with symbolic elements, inviting viewers to explore the depths of their own imagination. His artworks have gained recognition for their distinctive style and emotional impact, and he continues to be a prominent figure in the contemporary art scene.

Paul Cézanne: Painter - Paul Cézanne was a French post-impressionist painter known for his landscape art and genre paintings. He was a pioneer in modern art and is often referred to as the "father of modern painting." Cézanne's works are characterized by their bold use of color, innovative compositions, and meticulous attention to form and structure. He was known for his exploration of the relationship between color and form, creating a unique visual language that pushed the boundaries of traditional artistic conventions. Cézanne's landscapes often depict the serene beauty of the French countryside, while his genre paintings capture scenes of everyday life with a fresh and modern perspective. His innovative approach to painting had a profound impact on the art world and laid the groundwork for the development of modern art movements.

Camille Pissarro: Painter - Camille Pissarro was a Danish-French painter known for his landscape art and his role as a leading figure in the Impressionist movement. He was known for his innovative use of color, light, and atmospheric effects in his paintings, as well as his keen observation of nature. Pissarro's works are characterized by their loose brushwork, vibrant colors, and emphasis on capturing the changing effects of light in the natural world. He was known for his diverse range of subjects, including rural and urban landscapes, as well as scenes of everyday life in the French countryside. Pissarro's artworks are highly regarded for their technical skill, artistic innovation, and contributions to the Impressionist movement.

Erin Hanson: Artist - Erin Hanson is a contemporary American artist known for her vibrant and expressive landscape paintings. She is known for her unique style called "Open Impressionism," which combines elements of traditional impressionism with a more modern and abstract approach. Hanson's works are characterized by their bold and vibrant colors, dynamic brushwork, and energetic compositions that capture the beauty and essence of her artwork.

Raphael: Mythological painting, Allegory - Raphael was an Italian High Renaissance painter known for his masterful mythological and allegorical paintings. He was renowned for his technical skill, attention to detail, and ability to convey complex narratives through his art. Raphael's mythological paintings often depicted scenes from Greek and Roman mythology, showcasing his deep understanding of classical literature and his ability to capture the human form with grace and beauty. His allegorical works were known for their symbolism and allegorical representations of virtues and ideals. Raphael's works continue to be celebrated for their artistic excellence and profound storytelling.

Steve Henderson: Designer - Steve Henderson is a contemporary American designer known for his innovative and functional designs. He is known for his expertise in various fields of design, including graphic design, industrial design, and interior design. Henderson's designs are characterized by their sleek and modern aesthetic, attention to detail, and practicality. He is known for his ability to create visually stunning and user-friendly designs that enhance the user's experience while seamlessly integrating with their environment. Henderson's innovative designs have gained recognition in the design industry and have been used in various commercial and residential settings.

Pablo Picasso: Sculptor, Painter - Pablo Picasso was a Spanish artist known for his groundbreaking contributions to modern art. He was a prolific painter and sculptor, known for his innovative and avant-garde approach to art. Picasso's works are characterized by their bold use of color, abstract forms, and unique perspectives. He is credited with co-founding the Cubist movement, which shattered traditional artistic conventions and revolutionized the way art is perceived and created. Picasso's sculptures are known for their abstract and experimental forms, often pushing the boundaries of traditional sculpture. His paintings are equally renowned for their distinct style and artistic ingenuity, making him one of the most influential artists of the 20th century.

Caspar David Friedrich: Landscape art, German Romanticism - Caspar David Friedrich was a German painter known for his landscape art and his role as a leading figure in the Romantic movement. He is known for his deep connection with nature and his ability to convey a sense of spirituality and emotional depth in his landscapes. Friedrich's works are characterized by their dramatic and sublime landscapes, often depicting solitary figures in contemplative poses, showcasing his unique combination of naturalistic detail and emotional intensity. His landscapes are known for their deep emotional impact and their exploration of the relationship between man and nature, making him a prominent figure in the German Romantic movement.

Ansel Adams: Artsy Artist ID, Artsy - Ansel Adams was an American photographer known for his iconic landscape photographs of the American West. He is considered one of the greatest landscape photographers of all time and is renowned for his technical mastery, attention to detail, and profound sense of composition. Adams' works are characterized by their breathtaking views, precise exposure and focus, and meticulous darkroom techniques. He was known for his advocacy of environmental conservation and his ability to capture the awe-inspiring beauty of nature through his lens. Adams' photographs continue to be celebrated for their artistic and environmental significance.

Diego Rivera: Muralist, Museum of Modern Art Online Collection - Diego Rivera was a Mexican painter known for his large-scale murals that depicted the history, culture, and social issues of Mexico. He was a prominent figure in the Mexican muralism movement, which aimed to create public art that could educate and inspire the masses. Rivera's murals are characterized by their monumental size, bold use of color, and powerful social commentary. His works often depicted scenes of labor, revolution, and the struggles of the working class, showcasing his commitment to social and political activism. Rivera's murals can be found in various public buildings, museums, and institutions, including the Museum of Modern Art online collection.

Steve McCurry: Photographer- Steve McCurry is an American photographer known for his captivating and emotive images that capture the beauty, diversity, and humanity of cultures around the world. He is renowned for his documentary-style photography, which often focuses on people and their everyday lives in different parts of the world. McCurry's works are characterized by their powerful storytelling, vivid colors, and striking compositions. He has traveled extensively to remote and conflict-ridden regions, capturing images that reflect the human condition and the universal emotions that connect us all. McCurry's photographs have been widely published and exhibited, earning him numerous awards and accolades for his exceptional talent and commitment to visual storytelling.

Bob Ross: Landscape Art, Painter - Bob Ross was an American painter and television personality known for his serene landscape paintings and his popular instructional TV show "The Joy of Painting." Ross's distinctive style featured soft, muted landscapes with happy trees, fluffy clouds, and serene lakes, created using his unique wet-on-wet oil painting technique. His paintings were known for their tranquil and calming effect, inspiring many to take up painting as a hobby. Ross's warm and gentle personality, along with his artistic talent, made him a beloved figure in the art world, and his legacy continues to inspire and influence artists today.

John Atkinson Grimshaw: Mythological Painting, Landscape Art - John Atkinson Grimshaw was a British painter known for his atmospheric landscape paintings and mythological scenes. He was known for his meticulous attention to detail and his ability to capture the play of light and shadow in his works. Grimshaw's landscapes often depicted moonlit streets, misty harbors, and serene countryside scenes, creating a sense of mystery and enchantment. He also painted mythological scenes, often incorporating elements of nature and the supernatural in his compositions. Grimshaw's works were highly regarded during his time and continue to be admired for their technical skill and evocative mood.

Rob Gonsalves: Magic Realism, Painter - Rob Gonsalves is a Canadian painter known for his unique style of magic realism, which combines elements of fantasy, surrealism, and optical illusion in his works. His paintings often depict dreamlike scenes that challenge the viewer's perception and invite them to explore the boundaries between reality and imagination. Gonsalves' works are characterized by their intricate details, masterful use of light and shadow, and seamless blending of different realities in a single composition. His paintings are often whimsical and thought-provoking, inviting the viewer to interpret and interpret his fantastical worlds.

Paul Gauguin: Landscape Art, Tate Artist ID - Paul Gauguin was a French Post-Impressionist painter known for his bold use of color, innovative compositions, and exotic subject matter. He is considered one of the most influential artists of his time, known for his contributions to the Symbolist and Synthetist movements in art. Gauguin's landscapes often depicted the lush and vibrant landscapes of Tahiti and other South Pacific islands, showcasing his fascination with non-European cultures and his quest for spiritual and artistic inspiration. Gauguin's works are characterized by their vivid colors, simplified forms, and emotional intensity, reflecting his unique artistic vision and his innovative approach to painting.

James Tissot: Realism, Japonisme - James Tissot was a French painter known for his detailed and realistic depictions of contemporary life, often capturing the social customs and fashion of the Victorian era. He was also influenced by the Japanese art movement known as Japonisme, which had a significant impact on his style and subject matter. Tissot's works often portrayed scenes from daily life, including elegant society gatherings, fashionable women, and leisurely pastimes, showcasing his meticulous attention to detail and his ability to capture the nuances of human behavior. His works are known for their richness in narrative and his skillful use of light and shadow, as well as the incorporation of Japanese elements such as kimono patterns, fans, and screens, which reflect his fascination with Japanese aesthetics and culture.

Edouard Manet: Landscape Art, Genre Painting - Edouard Manet was a French painter and one of the leading figures of the Impressionist movement. He is known for his innovative approach to painting, challenging traditional artistic conventions and paving the way for modern art. Manet's works often depicted everyday scenes from urban life, including cafes, bars, and street scenes, as well as landscapes that captured the changing light and atmosphere of the city. His paintings are characterized by their bold brushwork, unconventional compositions, and a fresh and contemporary approach to color and form. Manet's works were considered controversial in his time, but they had a significant influence on the development of modern art and continue to be celebrated for their groundbreaking approach to depicting contemporary life.

Alphonse Mucha: Symbolism, Poster Artist - Alphonse Mucha was a Czech Art Nouveau painter and decorative artist known for his iconic posters and illustrations. Mucha's works are characterized by their intricate and decorative style, often featuring graceful female figures, intricate floral motifs, and richly ornamented frames. He was a prominent figure in the Symbolist movement, which aimed to express the emotional and spiritual aspects of human experience through art. Mucha's posters, in particular, are highly regarded for their exquisite craftsmanship, innovative design, and their ability to convey a sense of elegance, beauty, and mystique. His distinctive style has had a lasting impact on the world of art and design, and his works are still highly sought after by collectors and art enthusiasts alike.

Alfred Sisley: Painter, Still Life - Alfred Sisley was a French Impressionist painter known for his atmospheric landscapes and delicate still life paintings. He is considered one of the founding members of the Impressionist movement, known for his ability to capture the fleeting effects of light and atmosphere in his works. Sisley's landscapes often depicted the natural beauty of the French countryside, with its rivers, meadows, and trees, and his still life paintings showcased his skillful handling of color, light, and texture. His works are characterized by their softness, luminosity, and a keen sense of observation of nature. Despite facing financial struggles and lack of recognition during his lifetime, Sisley's works are now highly regarded for their poetic and evocative depictions of the natural world.

Fabian Perez: Painter - Fabian Perez is an Argentine figurative painter known for his captivating and emotive portraits and depictions of the tango dance. His works often portray the sensuality, passion, and mystique of the tango, capturing the dynamic movements and intimate connections between the dancers. Perez's paintings are characterized by their bold use of color, dramatic lighting, and his ability to convey deep emotions through his subjects' facial expressions and body language. His works have gained international recognition and are highly sought after by collectors and art enthusiasts for their powerful and evocative depictions of human emotions and the art of tango.

Gustave Courbet: Realism, Landscape Art - Gustave Courbet was a French painter and one of the leading figures of the Realist movement in art. He is known for his uncompromising and unapologetic approach to depicting reality, often focusing on the everyday lives of ordinary people and the natural world. Courbet's landscapes are characterized by their raw and honest depictions of nature, showcasing his keen observation of the changing light, atmosphere, and textures of the natural environment. He was known for his bold brushwork, earthy color palette, and his rejection of idealized and romantic depictions of nature. Courbet's works often challenged the conventional notions of beauty in art, as he sought to portray the truth and reality of the world around him.

Zaha Hadid: Architectural Painting, Architect - Zaha Hadid was a pioneering Iraqi-British architect and designer, known for her innovative and futuristic designs. She was the first woman to receive the prestigious Pritzker Architecture Prize, and her works have left a significant mark on the field of architecture. Hadid's architectural paintings, which are often seen as works of art in their own right, reflect her unique and visionary approach to design. Her paintings are characterized by their bold and dynamic use of form, color, and perspective, often blurring the boundaries between art and architecture. Hadid's designs are known for their avant-garde aesthetics, pushing the boundaries of what is possible in architectural design and challenging traditional notions of space, form, and function.

Jean-Léon Gérôme: Academic Art, Neo-Pompeian - Jean-Léon Gérôme was a French painter and sculptor known for his academic style and his depictions of historical and Orientalist subjects. He was a prominent figure in the Academic art movement, which emphasized precise draftsmanship, technical skill, and historical accuracy. Gérôme's works often portrayed scenes from ancient Rome and Pompeii, reflecting his fascination with classical art and architecture. His paintings are characterized by their meticulous attention to detail, rich color palette, and a sense of idealized beauty. Gérôme's works also had a neo-Pompeian influence, depicting scenes of everyday life and leisure in a classical setting, with an emphasis on sensuality and exoticism.

Carl Larsson: Landscape Art, Genre Painting - Carl Larsson was a Swedish painter known for his charming and idyllic depictions of Swedish rural life and his interior scenes of family life. His works are characterized by their warm and vibrant color palette, attention to detail, and a sense of intimacy and domesticity. Larsson's landscapes often portrayed the picturesque beauty of the Swedish countryside, with its rolling hills, lakes, and forests, while his genre paintings depicted the joys and simplicity of everyday family life. His works are highly regarded for their skillful compositions, realistic depictions of light and shadow, and their ability to capture the warmth and coziness of the home.

Mary Cassatt: Landscape Art, Genre Painting - Mary Cassatt was an American painter and printmaker known for her Impressionist works, particularly her depictions of women and children. She often painted landscapes, capturing the beauty of the natural world in her unique style. Cassatt's landscape paintings are characterized by their loose brushwork, delicate use of color, and attention to light and atmosphere. Her genre paintings, which often portrayed women and children in domestic settings, are known for their intimate and tender depictions, reflecting her deep understanding of the complexities of human relationships.

Sandro Botticelli: Mythological Painting, Early Renaissance - Sandro Botticelli was an Italian painter of the Early Renaissance period, known for his iconic mythological and allegorical works. His paintings often depicted scenes from classical mythology and ancient literature, with a focus on idealized figures and symbolic imagery. Botticelli's mythological paintings are characterized by their graceful and flowing lines, delicate use of color, and exquisite attention to detail. His works, such as "The Birth of Venus" and "Primavera," are considered masterpieces of Renaissance art, and they continue to captivate audiences with their beauty and allegorical meanings.

Daniel Ridgway Knight: Genre Painting, Landscape Art - Daniel Ridgway Knight was an American painter known for his genre paintings and landscapes, particularly his depictions of peasant life in France. His works often portrayed rural scenes, capturing the everyday life and customs of the French countryside. Knight's genre paintings are characterized by their meticulous attention to detail, realistic depictions of light and shadow, and warm color palette. His landscape paintings are known for their serene and peaceful atmosphere, depicting the beauty of nature in a tranquil and pastoral manner.

Joaquín Sorolla: Portrait, Impressionism - Joaquín Sorolla was a Spanish painter known for his vibrant and luminous Impressionist works, particularly his portraits. He was known for his skillful use of light and color, capturing the essence of his subjects and their surroundings with bold and confident brushwork. Sorolla's portraits are characterized by their lively and spontaneous style, often depicting people in everyday situations or capturing their personalities and emotions. His works are known for their vibrant color palette, evocative atmosphere, and masterful technique.

Andy Warhol: Portrait, Pop Art - Andy Warhol was an American artist known for his pioneering work in the Pop Art movement. He was known for his iconic portraits of celebrities and everyday objects, often depicting them in bold and vibrant colors with a distinctively graphic and stylized approach. Warhol's portraits are characterized by their bold and graphic style, often incorporating elements of popular culture and consumerism. His works challenged traditional notions of art and celebrity, and his innovative use of color, composition, and subject matter had a profound impact on contemporary art.

Kehinde Wiley: Painter, Contemporary Art - Kehinde Wiley is an American artist known for his bold and provocative works that challenge conventional representations of race, power, and identity. His paintings often feature African American subjects in heroic and regal poses, drawing inspiration from classical European portraiture. Wiley's works are characterized by their vivid and elaborate backgrounds, rich use of color, and meticulous attention to detail. His paintings are known for their powerful and thought-provoking narratives, addressing issues of race, gender, and representation in contemporary society.

Alfred Eisenstaedt: Photographer, Portrait - Alfred Eisenstaedt was a German-born American photographer known for his iconic portraits and photojournalism work. He was known for his candid and intimate portraits of notable figures, capturing their personalities and emotions with his camera. Eisenstaedt's portraits are characterized by their spontaneous and candid nature, often capturing a fleeting moment or expression that reveals the essence of the subject. His use of composition, lighting, and timing created memorable and timeless portraits that captured the humanity of his subjects, whether they were famous personalities or everyday people.

Gustav Klimt: Landscape Art, Religious Art - Gustav Klimt was an Austrian painter known for his richly decorative and symbolist works. He was known for his landscapes that often featured lush and vibrant scenes of nature, capturing the beauty of the world in a sensual and decorative manner. Klimt's religious art, particularly his murals and frescoes, often depicted biblical and allegorical themes with a distinctively ornamental and intricate style. His works are characterized by their intricate and elaborate use of gold leaf, bold patterns, and symbolism, creating mystical and otherworldly atmospheres.

Dante Gabriel Rossetti: Figurative Art, Allegory - Dante Gabriel Rossetti was an English painter, poet, and leader of the Pre-Raphaelite Brotherhood, known for his figurative art and allegorical works. He was known for his lush and detailed depictions of women, often with symbolic elements and allegorical meanings. Rossetti's figurative art is characterized by its meticulous attention to detail, rich use of color, and sensuous portrayal of his subjects. His allegorical works often explored themes of love, spirituality, and mythology, creating evocative and mysterious narratives that captivate viewers.

Tom Thomson: Landscape Art, Painter - Tom Thomson was a Canadian painter known for his vivid and expressive landscape paintings, often depicting the rugged wilderness of Canada. He was a prominent member of the Group of Seven, a group of Canadian artists who sought to capture the beauty of the Canadian landscape in their works. Thomson's landscape art is characterized by its bold and vibrant use of color, loose brushwork, and emotional intensity. His paintings often evoke a sense of awe and reverence for the natural world, capturing the untamed wilderness of Canada with a sense of awe and admiration.

Edgar Degas: Genre Painting, Impressionism - Edgar Degas was a French artist known for his innovative works in the Impressionist movement, particularly his genre paintings. He was known for his depictions of everyday life, often focusing on ballet dancers, horse races, and other scenes of modern urban life. Degas' genre paintings are characterized by their dynamic compositions, skillful use of color, and unique perspectives. His works often capture fleeting moments and reveal the human form in motion, creating a sense of spontaneity and vitality.

Utagawa Hiroshige: Landscape Art, Painter - Utagawa Hiroshige was a Japanese ukiyo-e artist known for his landscape prints, particularly his series "The Fifty-three Stations of the Tokaido." He was known for his depictions of the Japanese landscape, capturing the beauty of nature in a poetic and evocative manner. Hiroshige's landscape art is characterized by his mastery of composition, use of color, and ability to convey a sense of mood and atmosphere. His works often depict scenes of daily life, capturing the cultural and natural beauty of Japan with a sense of harmony and tranquility.

Camille Corot: Realism, Landscape Art - Camille Corot was a French painter known for his landscape paintings, particularly his innovative approach to plein air painting. He was a key figure in the development of the Barbizon School, a group of artists who focused on painting the natural landscape in a realistic and direct manner. Corot's landscape art is characterized by his subtle and delicate use of color, soft and hazy atmospheres, and poetic depiction of nature. His works often convey a sense of serenity and contemplation, capturing the beauty of the French countryside with a sense of reverence and admiration.

Edward Steichen: Photographer, Pictorialism - Edward Steichen was an American photographer known for his pioneering work in pictorialism, a photographic movement that aimed to elevate photography to the level of fine art. Steichen's photographs were characterized by their soft focus, atmospheric lighting, and emotive qualities, often resembling paintings or etchings. He was known for his portraits, landscapes, and still life photographs, which conveyed a sense of emotional depth and artistic expression. Steichen's photographs often featured dreamlike and poetic compositions, blurring the lines between reality and imagination, and pushing the boundaries of what photography could achieve as an artistic medium.

David Hockney: Digital Art, Graphics - David Hockney is a British artist known for his innovative work in digital art and graphics. He has been at the forefront of using technology in art, experimenting with various mediums and techniques, including iPad and computer-generated art. Hockney's digital art is characterized by his bold use of color, playful compositions, and vibrant visuals. He has pushed the boundaries of traditional art forms through his experimentation with technology, creating unique and visually stunning works that challenge the notions of traditional artistic mediums.

Ivan Aivazovsky: Mythological Painting, Landscape Art - Ivan Aivazovsky was a Russian painter known for his breathtaking seascapes, marine paintings, and mythological works. He was known for his depictions of the sea in all its moods, capturing the power and majesty of the ocean with astonishing detail and skill. Aivazovsky's mythological paintings often featured scenes from ancient Greek mythology, depicting gods, goddesses, and mythological creatures with a sense of drama and awe. His landscape art is characterized by his mastery of light and atmosphere, creating stunning visual effects that bring the sea and the natural world to life on canvas.

Josephine Wall: Painter, Fantasy - Josephine Wall is a British artist known for her enchanting and whimsical paintings that transport viewers to a fantastical world of imagination. Her works often feature dreamlike and surreal scenes, filled with mythical creatures, fairies, and magical landscapes. Wall's paintings are characterized by their intricate details, rich use of color, and imaginative compositions. Her works evoke a sense of wonder and evoke the magic of fairy tales, creating a sense of escape into a world of fantasy and imagination.

Peter Paul Rubens: Mythological Painting, Landscape Art - Peter Paul Rubens was a Flemish Baroque painter known for his dynamic and grandiose works, particularly his mythological paintings and landscape art. He was known for his dramatic compositions, bold use of color, and skillful depiction of human anatomy. Rubens' mythological paintings often depicted scenes from Greek and Roman mythology, portraying gods, goddesses, and heroes in epic and theatrical ways. His landscape art is characterized by his skillful rendering of nature, capturing the beauty and grandeur of the natural world with a sense of awe and admiration.

Henri Rousseau: Landscape Art, Figure Painting - Henri Rousseau, also known as "Le Douanier" (the customs officer), was a French Post-Impressionist painter known for his naive and dreamlike works. His landscape art often featured lush and exotic scenes, often imagined rather than based on direct observation. Rousseau's figure paintings were characterized by his stylized and imaginative depictions of people and animals, often set in fantastical or surreal settings. His works were known for their bold use of color, flattened perspective, and unique compositions that conveyed a sense of wonder and mystery.

Edward Burne-Jones: Mythological Painting, Genre Painting - Edward Burne-Jones was a British painter associated with the Pre-Raphaelite movement, known for his mythological paintings and genre works. He was known for his idealized and romanticized depictions of figures from myth, legend and folklore, often portraying them in a mystical and symbolic manner. Burne-Jones' mythological paintings were characterized by their ethereal beauty, intricate details, and rich use of color. His genre paintings often depicted scenes from everyday life, often with a touch of romance or whimsy, and were known for their evocative storytelling and emotional depth. Burne-Jones' works often conveyed a sense of otherworldly beauty and a longing for a fantastical realm, blurring the boundaries between reality and imagination.

Pixar- Pixar is a renowned animation studio known for its groundbreaking films that have redefined the animation industry. Their innovative use of computer-generated imagery

(CGI) has brought to life beloved characters and stories, creating memorable films that have captured the hearts of audiences worldwide. Pixar films are known for their visually stunning landscapes, imaginative worlds, and emotionally resonant storytelling, making them a significant force in the world of animated art.

Alexander McQueen was a British fashion designer known for his avant-garde and boundary-pushing designs. He was known for his bold and daring approach to fashion, incorporating elements of surrealism, romanticism, and historical references into his designs. McQueen's work often challenged traditional notions of fashion and beauty, pushing the boundaries of what was considered acceptable in the industry. His innovative and visionary designs continue to influence and inspire the world of fashion.

Anders Zorn was a Swedish painter known for his landscape art and marine art. He was celebrated for his ability to capture the play of light and shadow in his paintings, creating breathtaking scenes of nature that are both realistic and atmospheric. Zorn's works often featured serene and peaceful landscapes, with a particular focus on water, which he portrayed with remarkable skill and precision.

Jean Auguste Dominique Ingres was a French painter known for his romanticism and neoclassical style. He was highly regarded for his exquisite draftsmanship, meticulous attention to detail, and his ability to convey a sense of idealized beauty in his paintings. Ingres' works often featured mythological and allegorical subjects, with a focus on the human form and its graceful contours. His paintings were characterized by their classical composition, refined technique, and emotional depth.

Franz Xaver Winterhalter was a German painter known for his landscape art and academic art. He was renowned for his portraits of royalty and aristocracy, capturing the opulence and elegance of the Victorian era. Winterhalter's works were marked by their attention to detail, exquisite craftsmanship, and ability to capture the essence of his subjects with great precision.

Katsushika Hokusai was a Japanese artist known for his japonisme and portrait art. He is famous for his iconic woodblock print series "Thirty-six Views of Mount Fuji," which includes his most famous work, "The Great Wave off Kanagawa." Hokusai's works were characterized by their bold compositions, intricate details, and dramatic use of color and contrast. His depictions of landscapes and nature, as well as his portraits of people, have had a profound impact on art and continue to be celebrated today.

John Constable was an English painter known for his realism and landscape art. He is considered one of the greatest landscape painters in the history of Western art, with his works often depicting the beauty and tranquility of the English countryside. Constable's paintings were characterized by their meticulous attention to detail, rich use of color, and atmospheric effects that captured the changing moods of nature.

Canaletto was an Italian painter known for his landscape art, particularly his depictions of Venice. He was celebrated for his precise and detailed renderings of architecture and cityscapes, capturing the grandeur and beauty of Venice's iconic landmarks. Canaletto's works were characterized by their intricate compositions, skillful use of perspective, and masterful handling of light and shadow.

Shepard Fairey is an American graffiti artist known for his contemporary art and social commentary. He gained worldwide recognition for his iconic "Hope" poster during Barack Obama's 2008 presidential campaign, which became a symbol of optimism and change. Fairey's works often incorporate political and social messages, addressing issues such as power, inequality, and the environment. His distinctive style, characterized by bold graphics, vibrant colors, and provocative imagery, has made him a prominent figure in the street art and contemporary art world.

Gordon Parks was an American film director and photographer known for his social realism and documentary-style works. He was a trailblazer in his use of photography and film to address social issues such as poverty, discrimination, and civil rights, capturing the struggles and stories of marginalized communities. Parks' works were characterized by their powerful storytelling, humanistic approach, and raw emotional impact.

George Inness was an American painter known for his landscape art and depictions of the American countryside. He was celebrated for his ability to capture the beauty and spirituality of nature in his paintings, creating serene and contemplative scenes that often had a mystical quality. Inness' works were characterized by their poetic compositions, soft tonalities, and atmospheric effects, conveying a sense of quietude and harmony.

Anthony van Dyck was a Flemish painter known for his mythological paintings and allegories. He was a prominent portrait painter during the Baroque period, known for his ability to capture the likeness and personality of his subjects with great skill and sensitivity. Van Dyck's works were characterized by their rich color palettes, dramatic lighting, and expressive brushwork, creating vivid and lifelike portrayals of mythological and allegorical themes.

Vivian Maier was an American street photographer known for her captivating and candid portraits of people and street scenes. Her works were discovered posthumously and have gained widespread recognition for their unique perspective on everyday life in urban America. Maier's photographs were characterized by their striking compositions, insightful observations, and keen eye for capturing the human element in her subjects.

Catrin Welz-Stein is a contemporary digital artist known for her imaginative and whimsical artworks. She creates surreal and dreamlike collages by combining elements from different sources, creating visually stunning and thought-provoking compositions. Welz-Stein's works often feature fantastical landscapes, intriguing characters, and rich symbolism, inviting viewers into her imaginative world.

Lawren Harris was a Canadian painter known for his landscape art and depictions of the Canadian wilderness. He was a member of the Group of Seven, a group of Canadian artists who sought to capture the unique beauty and spirit of the Canadian landscape. Harris' works were characterized by their bold use of color, simplified forms, and abstracted compositions, creating powerful and evocative portrayals of the Canadian wilderness.

Salvador Dali was a Spanish surrealist painter known for his landscape art and allegorical works. He was a prominent figure in the surrealist movement, known for his eccentric and fantastical imagery that pushed the boundaries of reality and explored the depths of the subconscious mind. Dali's works were characterized by their meticulous details, juxtaposition of unrelated objects, and surreal and dreamlike elements that challenged conventional notions of art and reality.

David Bowie was a British musician and artist known for his influential contributions to rock music and his distinctive style. He was also an accomplished painter and art collector, known for his passion for contemporary art and his support of emerging artists. Bowie's paintings were characterized by their bold and expressive brushwork, vibrant colors, and abstracted compositions, reflecting his unique creative vision and artistic sensibilities.

Agnes Cecile is an Italian contemporary artist known for her expressive and emotive artworks. She specializes in portraiture, creating deeply emotional and introspective paintings that explore the complexities of human emotions and the human experience. Agnes Cecile's works are characterized by their raw and vulnerable depictions of the human form, their bold use of color and texture, and their profound emotional impact.

Titian was an Italian painter known for his mythological paintings and his contributions to the Venetian school of art. He was a master of color and composition, known for his dynamic and emotionally charged depictions of myth ological themes and allegories. Titian's works were characterized by their rich and luminous color palette, masterful handling of light and shadow, and exquisite attention to detail. His paintings often conveyed a sense of drama, emotion, and sensual beauty, making him one of the most influential painters of his time.

Martin Johnson Heade was an American painter known for his landscape art and marine art. He was renowned for his depictions of the natural world, particularly the landscapes and seascapes of the American East Coast and South America. Heade's works were characterized by their meticulous attention to detail, vivid coloration, and atmospheric effects, capturing the beauty and serenity of the natural world in his paintings.

Scott Naismith is a contemporary Scottish painter known for his vibrant and expressive landscape art. His works are characterized by bold and dynamic brushstrokes, rich color palettes, and a sense of energy and movement. Naismith's landscapes often depict the stunning natural beauty of Scotland and other scenic locations, capturing the play of light and the ever-changing moods of the environment.

William Morris was a British artist, designer, and writer who was a leading figure in the Arts and Crafts movement. He was known for his decorative arts, including textiles, wallpaper, and furniture, which were characterized by intricate patterns, natural motifs, and a focus on craftsmanship and handwork. Morris believed that art and design should be accessible to all and sought to create beautiful and functional objects that could enhance people's daily lives.

Berthe Morisot was a French painter and one of the few prominent female artists of the Impressionist movement. She is known for her delicate and sensitive portraits, often depicting women and children in intimate domestic settings. Morisot's works were characterized by their loose brushwork, soft color palette, and ability to capture the fleeting effects of light and atmosphere.

Vladimir Kush is a contemporary Russian painter known for his surreal and fantastical artworks. His paintings often feature dreamlike landscapes, whimsical creatures, and symbolic elements that evoke a sense of mystery and wonder. Kush's works are characterized by their intricate details, imaginative compositions, and a blending of reality and fantasy.

William Holman Hunt was an English painter and one of the founding members of the Pre-Raphaelite Brotherhood, a group of artists who rebelled against the academic conventions of their time and sought to revive the purity and sincerity of early Renaissance art. Hunt's works were often characterized by their detailed and meticulous technique, vivid coloration, and deep symbolism, with a focus on religious and mythological subjects.

Edvard Munch was a Norwegian painter and one of the most important figures in the expressionist movement. He is best known for his haunting and emotionally charged works, including his famous painting "The Scream." Munch's works were characterized by their bold and intense brushwork, dramatic use of color, and powerful depictions of human emotions and psychological states.

Joseph Mallord William Turner was an English painter known for his innovative and groundbreaking approach to landscape art and marine art. He is considered one of the greatest landscape painters in Western art history and is known for his ability to capture the sublime beauty and power of nature. Turner's works were characterized by their atmospheric effects, luminous color palette, and dramatic compositions that pushed the boundaries of traditional landscape painting.

Gustave Doré was a French artist known for his romantic and allegorical illustrations. He is best known for his intricate and detailed engravings, which often depicted scenes from literature, mythology, and religious texts. Doré's works were characterized by their dramatic and imaginative compositions, skillful use of light and shadow, and intricate details that brought his subjects to life.

Thomas Eakins was an American realist painter known for his depictions of everyday life and his meticulous attention to detail. He is considered one of the most important figures in the development of American art and is known for his portraits, genre scenes, and art of painting. Eakins' works were characterized by their technical precision, naturalism, and a deep sense of human observation.

Ilya Repin was a Russian realist painter known for his genre scenes and portraits. He is considered one of the leading figures of the Russian realist art movement and is known for his ability to capture the everyday lives of ordinary people with sensitivity and compassion. Repin's works were characterized by their detailed and naturalistic style, rich color palette, and emotional depth.

Amedeo Modigliani was an Italian painter known for his distinctive style of portrait painting. Modigliani's works are characterized by elongated figures, simplified forms, and stylized features, often with elongated necks and faces. He was known for his ability to capture the essence and personality of his subjects through his unique and expressive style, which often conveyed a sense of melancholy and introspection.

Johannes Vermeer was a Dutch painter known for his genre paintings and portraits. He is considered one of the greatest painters of the Dutch Golden Age and is known for his ability to capture the play of light and his meticulous attention to detail. Vermeer's works were characterized by their carefully composed scenes, use of natural light, and refined technique, often depicting everyday life and domestic interiors.

Eyvind Earle was an American painter known for his landscape art. He is best known for his stylized and colorful depictions of nature, often featuring rolling hills, towering trees, and serene landscapes. Earle's works were characterized by their bold and vibrant use of color, simplified forms, and a sense of harmony and balance.

Ivan Shishkin was a Russian realist painter known for his landscape art. He is considered one of the greatest landscape painters in Russian art history and is known for his ability to capture the beauty and tranquility of the Russian wilderness. Shishkin's works were characterized by their meticulous attention to detail, rich and varied color palette, and a deep sense of naturalism.

Rembrandt van Rijn was a Dutch painter and one of the most important figures in the history of Western art. He is known for his masterful use of light and shadow, his ability to convey deep emotion and psychological complexity in his portraits, and his innovative and experimental approach to painting. Rembrandt's works were characterized by their dramatic use of light, rich and expressive brushwork, and a deep understanding of human nature.

Gil Elvgren was an American painter known for his pin-up art. He is best known for his glamorous and sensual depictions of women, often in playful and flirtatious poses. Elvgren's works were characterized by their impeccable technique, attention to detail, and a sense of whimsy and fantasy.

Nicholas Roerich was a Russian painter known for his mythological and landscape art. He is best known for his depictions of the mystical and spiritual aspects of nature, often incorporating symbolic elements and esoteric themes. Roerich's works were characterized by their bold use of color, intricate compositions, and a sense of mysticism and spirituality.

Henri Matisse was a French painter and one of the most important figures in modern art. He is known for his innovative use of color, bold and expressive brushwork, and his pioneering role in the development of Fauvism. Matisse's works were characterized by their vibrant and bold color palette, simplified forms, and a sense of joy and exuberance.

Thomas Gainsborough was an English painter known for his landscape art and rococo style portraits. He is considered one of the most important landscape painters of the 18th century and is known for his ability to capture the natural beauty of the English countryside. Gainsborough's works were characterized by their atmospheric effects, rich color palette, and a sense of elegance and charm.

Artgerm, also known as Stanley Lau, is a contemporary digital artist and illustrator known for his dynamic and vibrant artworks. He is best known for his depictions of female characters, often with a strong sense of femininity, beauty, and empowerment. Artgerm's works are characterized by their stunning use of color, intricate details, and a sense of dynamic movement.

Studio Ghibli is a Japanese animation film studio known for its critically acclaimed and visually stunning animated films. Founded by Hayao Miyazaki and Isao Takahata, Studio Ghibli has produced numerous iconic and beloved films, including "My Neighbor Totoro," "Spirited Away," "Princess Mononoke," and "Howl's Moving Castle," among others. Studio Ghibli films are known for their breathtaking hand-drawn animation, rich and imaginative storytelling, and deeply emotional and resonant themes that often explore the relationships between humans, nature, and technology. The studio's films have garnered worldwide acclaim for their artistic excellence and have left a lasting impact on the animation industry and popular culture.

Grant Wood, known for his landscape art and association with the regionalism art movement, is remembered for his iconic painting "American Gothic," which depicts a farmer and his daughter in front of a farmhouse. His works often depicted rural American life, capturing the essence of the American Midwest with its landscapes, people, and traditions.

Jeremy Mann, on the other hand, is a contemporary artist known for his research-based approach to painting. His works often explore urban landscapes and cityscapes, capturing the mood, atmosphere, and energy of urban environments through his unique style and technique.

Mark Keathley is an American painter known for his breathtaking landscapes, particularly those that capture the beauty of nature and the serenity of outdoor scenes. His works often feature majestic mountains, tranquil lakes, and lush forests, inviting viewers to connect with the natural world.

Maxfield Parrish, a renowned American artist from the late 19th and early 20th centuries, is known for his genre art and mythological paintings. His works often feature dreamlike and ethereal scenes, characterized by luminous colors, rich details, and a sense of otherworldliness.

Andrew Wyeth, a prominent realist artist, is known for his landscape art that captures the beauty and complexity of the rural American countryside. His works often feature stark and evocative scenes, depicting the interplay of light and shadow, and the emotional resonance of the landscape.

RHADS, also known as Rhads, is a contemporary artist known for his bold and colorful abstract art. His works often feature vibrant and expressive brushstrokes, creating dynamic and visually captivating compositions that invite viewers to interpret and connect with the artwork on a personal level.

David Lynch, known for his contributions to independent cinema in the USA, is a filmmaker and artist known for his unique blend of magic realism and surrealist elements in his films. His works often explore the darker and mysterious aspects of human nature, presenting unconventional narratives and thought-provoking visuals.

Frederic Remington, a prominent American artist from the late 19th century, is known for his realistic depictions of the American West, particularly its landscapes and cowboy culture. His works often capture the ruggedness and grandeur of the Western frontier, showcasing the beauty and challenges of life in the wild west.

Jan Van Eyck, a master of the Northern Renaissance, is known for his genre painting and realistic depiction of everyday life. His works often feature meticulously detailed scenes, characterized by their technical precision, rich colors, and intricate compositions.

Mikko Lagerstedt is a Finnish fine art photographer known for his captivating landscapes and atmospheric scenes. His works often feature surreal and dreamlike elements, inviting viewers to explore the beauty and mystery of the natural world through his lens.

Banksy, a renowned contemporary artist and graffiti artist, is known for his thought-provoking and politically charged artworks that challenge societal norms and raise awareness about social and political issues. His works often feature bold and powerful messages, conveyed through his distinctive stencil-based style.

Michael Cheval, known for his imaginative and surreal artworks, is a contemporary artist known for his unique blend of fantasy and reality. His works often feature whimsical and theatrical scenes, characterized by their intricate details, playful compositions, and enigmatic narratives.

Anna Razumovskaya, a Russian-born artist, is known for her elegant and romantic depictions of women, often portrayed as graceful and sophisticated figures. Her works often feature flowing dresses, lush backgrounds, and a sense of beauty and femininity.

Jean-François Millet, a prominent artist of the Barbizon school and a genre painter, is known for his depictions of rural life and landscapes. His works often capture the daily activities of rural peasants and the beauty of the French countryside, portraying scenes with a sense of dignity and humanity Thomas W Schaller is a renowned watercolor artist known for his architectural and urban landscape paintings. His works often showcase the beauty and complexity of cityscapes, capturing the interplay of light and shadow, reflections, and atmospheric effects with a loose and expressive watercolor technique.

Charlie Bowater is a contemporary artist known for her digital paintings, particularly her captivating fantasy and character artworks. Her works often feature strong and dynamic female characters, portrayed with intricate details, rich colors, and a sense of fantasy and wonder.

El Greco, a master of the Spanish Renaissance, is known for his mythological paintings and landscape art. His works often exhibit his distinct style characterized by elongated figures, dramatic use of color and light, and a sense of spiritual and emotional intensity.

From Studio Ghibli, a renowned Japanese animation studio, artists such as Hayao Miyazaki and Isao Takahata have created breathtaking and enchanting worlds through their animated films. Their works often feature intricate hand-drawn animations, rich storytelling, and fantastical landscapes, capturing the imagination of audiences around the world.

Paolo Roversi is a renowned fashion and portrait photographer known for his unique and poetic style. His works often feature dreamlike and atmospheric images, with a focus on capturing the essence and personality of his subjects through his distinctive use of lighting, composition, and mood.

Carne Griffiths is an artist known for his intricate and delicate artworks created with unconventional mediums such as tea, ink, and alcohol. His works often blend elements of nature, portraiture, and abstraction, creating mesmerizing and ethereal compositions that evoke a sense of wonder and beauty.

Man Ray, a pioneer of avant-garde and Dada movements, is known for his abstract art and assemblage works. His innovative approach to art often involved combining ordinary objects and materials in unconventional ways, creating thought-provoking and visually intriguing compositions that challenge traditional artistic norms.

August Sander is a renowned German photographer known for his powerful portraits and documentary-style photography. His works often capture the human condition and the diverse faces of society, reflecting a deep sense of empathy and understanding of the human experience.

Andrew Macara is a painter known for his vibrant and dynamic landscapes, often depicting scenes of nature and the outdoors. His works are characterized by bold brushwork, rich colors, and a sense of energy and movement, capturing the beauty and spirit of the natural world.

Evelyn De Morgan was a prominent painter associated with the Pre-Raphaelite Brotherhood, known for her allegorical and symbolist works. Her paintings often feature rich and luminous colors, intricate details, and a sense of myth and mysticism, exploring themes of spirituality, feminism, and social justice.

William Blake was a visionary artist and poet known for his romanticism and allegorical works. His paintings and writings often depicted fantastical and symbolic imagery, exploring themes of spirituality, mythology, and the human condition.

Sally Mann is a contemporary photographer known for her landscape art and contemporary art photography. Her works often capture the beauty and mystery of the natural world, with a focus on the relationship between humans and their environment, and the passage of time.

Oleg Oprisco is a fine art photographer known for his surreal and conceptual works. His photographs often blend elements of fantasy, dreams, and storytelling, creating visually stunning and thought-provoking compositions that challenge reality and perception.

Yuumei is a visual artist known for her digital artworks that explore themes of nature, technology, and social issues. Her works often feature captivating and whimsical illustrations with a message of environmental conservation, social justice, and personal growth.

Helmut Newton was a renowned fashion and portrait photographer known for his provocative and iconic images. His works often featured strong and sensual portrayals of women, with a bold and provocative style that challenged traditional notions of femininity and beauty.

Henry Ossawa Tanner was an African American artist known for his realist and landscape art paintings. His works often depicted scenes of everyday life, with a focus on the African American experience and his own personal spiritual journey, capturing the beauty and dignity of his subjects with a sensitive and empathetic approach.

Asher Brown Durand was a prominent landscape artist associated with the Hudson River School, known for his panoramic and detailed landscapes. His works often depicted the beauty of the American wilderness, with a focus on the majestic landscapes of the Hudson River Valley and the Catskill Mountains.

TeamLab is a Japanese digital art collective known for their immersive and interactive artworks that blend art, technology, and nature. Their works often involve projection mapping, LED lights, and interactive elements, creating multi-sensory experiences that challenge traditional notions of art and space.

August Macke was a German painter known for his landscape art and colorful compositions. His works often depicted scenes of nature, with a focus on bold colors, expressive brushwork, and a sense of playfulness and joy,

Armand Guillaumin was a French Impressionist painter known for his vibrant and atmospheric landscapes. His works often depicted the changing effects of light and color in nature, capturing the beauty and fleeting moments of the natural world with loose brushstrokes and a keen eye for detail.

Terry Redlin was an American artist known for his nostalgic and serene depictions of rural landscapes and wildlife. His works often portrayed idyllic scenes of nature, evoking a sense of peace and tranquility, and resonating with a sense of nostalgia and Americana.

Antoine Blanchard was a French painter associated with the School of Paris, known for his charming and nostalgic depictions of Parisian street scenes. His works often featured romanticized views of Paris, capturing the beauty of the city's architecture, people, and daily life with a meticulous attention to detail and a warm color palette.

Anna Ancher was a Danish Impressionist painter known for her luminous and vibrant landscapes and domestic scenes. Her works often portrayed the everyday life of fishermen and farmers in the Danish countryside, capturing the play of light and color with a sensitive and atmospheric approach.

Ohara Koson was a Japanese printmaker known for his nihonga (Japanese-style painting) and exquisite woodblock prints. His works often depicted scenes of nature, including birds, flowers, and landscapes, with a delicate and intricate style that reflected his deep appreciation for the beauty of the natural world.

Walter Langley was a British painter associated with the Newlyn School, known for his poignant and emotive depictions of everyday life, particularly of working-class people. His works often portrayed scenes of fishermen, farmers, and their families, capturing the hardships, joys, and struggles of everyday life with a sensitive and compassionate approach.

Yayoi Kusama is a Japanese contemporary artist known for her abstract art and feminist art. Her works often feature bold and vibrant colors, repetitive patterns, and organic forms, exploring themes of identity, infinity, and the human psyche. Kusama is also known for her immersive installations and iconic polka dot motifs, which have become signature elements of her art.

Stan Lee was an American publisher and comic book writer, best known for co-creating many iconic superheroes, such as Spider-Man, Iron Man, and the X-Men, which have become beloved characters in popular culture.

Chuck Close is a contemporary artist known for his large-scale, hyperrealistic portraits. His works often depict friends, family, and fellow artists, capturing their likeness with incredible detail and precision. Close's unique approach to portraiture, utilizing grid-based techniques and unconventional materials, has made him a prominent figure in the art world.

Albert Edelfelt was a Finnish painter known for his realist style and depictions of everyday life in Finland. His works often portrayed landscapes, genre scenes, and historical subjects, capturing the natural beauty and cultural nuances of his homeland with a keen eye for detail and a masterful use of light and color.

Mark Seliger is an American photographer known for his celebrity portraits and editorial photography. His works have been featured in numerous magazines and have earned him recognition for his distinctive style and ability to capture the essence of his subjects.

Eugene Delacroix was a French painter known for his romantic and dramatic depictions of historical and mythological subjects. His works often featured dynamic compositions, vibrant colors, and emotional intensity, reflecting the spirit of Romanticism and revolutionizing the traditional approach to landscape art.

John Lavery was an Irish painter known for his portraits and depictions of social life in late 19th and early 20th century Britain. His works often portrayed influential figures of his time, including politicians, artists, and socialites, capturing their personalities and lifestyles with a skillful use of light, color, and composition.

Theo van Rysselberghe was a Belgian neo-impressionist painter known for his pointillist style and depictions of landscapes, seascapes, and figures. His works often featured vibrant colors, precise dots of paint, and a luminous quality, showcasing his mastery of the neo-impressionist technique.

Marc Chagall was a Russian-French artist known for his unique blend of landscape art, religious themes, and dreamlike imagery. His works often portrayed scenes from his childhood in Russia, Jewish folklore, and biblical stories, capturing the whimsical and poetic nature of his imagination with bold colors and surreal compositions.

Rolf Armstrong was an American painter known for his portraits of glamorous women, often depicted in pin-up style. His works captured the beauty and allure of feminine sensuality, with an emphasis on fashion, elegance, and glamour.

Brent Heighton is a Canadian artist known for his landscapes and urban scenes, capturing the beauty of nature and the charm of cityscapes with a loose and impressionistic style. His works often feature bold colors, expressive brushstrokes, and a sense of serenity and tranquility.

A.J. Casson was a Canadian painter and member of the Group of Seven, known for his landscape art and depictions of the Canadian wilderness. His works often portrayed the rugged beauty of the Canadian landscape, capturing the majestic vistas, changing seasons, and unique light with a distinctive style and sense of place.

Egon Schiele was an Austrian painter known for his expressive and provocative works, often depicting the human form in a distorted and allegorical manner. His works explored themes of sexuality, mortality, and the human condition, and his bold use of color and line has made him a prominent figure in the history of modern art.

Maximilien Luce was a French painter known for his pointillist style and depictions of landscapes, cityscapes, and social issues. His works often featured vibrant colors, precise dots of paint, and a sense of social consciousness, reflecting his political beliefs and his dedication to capturing the beauty of the world in a unique way.

Georges Seurat was a French painter known for his innovative pointillist technique and his depictions of landscapes and genre scenes. His works are characterized by small dots of color applied in a systematic manner, creating a sense of luminosity and optical vibrancy. Seurat's meticulous approach to color and composition, as well as his pioneering use of scientific color theory, has had a significant influence on the development of modern art.

George Frederic Watts was a British painter known for his symbolic and allegorical works, often dealing with themes of spirituality, social commentary, and the human condition. His works are characterized by a dramatic use of light and shadow, rich colors, and emotive expressions, reflecting his deep philosophical and humanitarian beliefs.

Arthur Hughes was an English painter and one of the leading members of the Pre-Raphaelite Brotherhood, a group of artists who sought to revive the aesthetic principles of the early Italian Renaissance. Hughes' works often depicted romantic and idealized scenes from literature and mythology, characterized by vibrant colors, meticulous attention to detail, and a dreamlike quality.

Anton Mauve was a Dutch painter and one of the prominent members of the Hague School, known for his atmospheric landscapes and genre scenes. His works often portrayed rural life in the Netherlands, capturing the changing seasons, the effects of light, and the everyday activities of the local people with a naturalistic and sensitive approach.

Lucian Freud was a British painter known for his distinctive style of figurative painting and his intimate and often raw depictions of the human form. His works are characterized by his bold use of color, thick and textured brushstrokes, and a keen psychological insight into the personalities of his subjects. Freud's works have been widely acclaimed for their powerful and emotional impact.

Jessie Willcox Smith was an American illustrator known for her charming and whimsical illustrations of children, often featured in magazines, books, and advertisements. Her works are characterized by their delicate and detailed renderings, capturing the innocence and wonder of childhood with a nostalgic and sentimental approach.

Leonardo da Vinci was an Italian painter, inventor, and polymath of the High Renaissance period, known for his exceptional skills in painting, sculpture, and engineering. His works, such as the iconic Mona Lisa and The Last Supper, are revered for their masterful technique, innovative compositions, and profound artistic vision, making him one of the greatest artists in history.

Edward John Poynter was a British painter known for his historical and mythological paintings, often depicting scenes from ancient history, literature, and classical mythology. His works are characterized by their meticulous attention to detail, rich colors, and a classical aesthetic, reflecting his deep knowledge and admiration for classical art and culture.

Brooke Shaden is a contemporary American photographer known for her conceptual and surreal imagery. Her works often portray dreamlike and fantastical scenes, exploring themes of self-expression, identity, and human emotions. Shaden's unique approach to photography, combining digital manipulation and fine art techniques, has earned her recognition as one of the leading artists in the field of conceptual photography.

J.M.W. Turner was a British landscape artist known for his groundbreaking approach to capturing the effects of light and atmosphere in his works. His paintings are characterized by their dramatic and evocative renderings of seascapes, landscapes, and marine scenes, often imbued with a sense of sublime and awe-inspiring beauty. Turner's innovative use of color, composition, and brushwork has had a significant influence on the development of landscape art and has earned him a reputation as one of the greatest painters of his time.

Wassily Kandinsky was a Russian painter and art theorist known for his pioneering work in abstract art and his role in the development of abstract expressionism. His works are characterized by their bold use of color, dynamic compositions, and spiritual themes, reflecting his belief that art should be pure and free from the constraints of representational forms. Kandinsky's innovative approach to painting, using abstract forms and colors to evoke emotions and spiritual experiences, has had a profound impact on the development of modern art and has earned him a reputation as one of the pioneers of abstract art.

Wes Anderson is a contemporary American film director known for his distinct visual style and unique storytelling approach. His films, such as "The Royal Tenenbaums," "Moonrise Kingdom," and "The Grand Budapest Hotel," are characterized by their meticulously crafted sets, carefully chosen color palettes, and whimsical narratives that often blend elements of comedy, drama, and nostalgia. Anderson's films are recognized for their distinctive aesthetics and quirky characters, making him one of the most influential directors in contemporary cinema.

Jean-Honoré Fragonard was an 18th-century French painter known for his romantic and idyllic landscapes. His works often depicted lush scenery, charming rural scenes, and playful allegories, characterized by his delicate brushwork, soft colors, and evocative compositions. Fragonard's works are recognized for their dreamlike quality and emotional appeal, capturing the beauty of nature and the fleeting moments of joy and romance.

Amanda Clark is a contemporary researcher known for her work in the field of art history and cultural studies. Her research often focuses on the intersection of art, culture, and society, examining how art reflects and shapes the world we live in. Clark's contributions to the field of art research have been recognized for their depth of analysis, critical thinking, and interdisciplinary approach.

Tom Roberts was an Australian artist and a leading member of the Heidelberg School, a group of artists known for their distinctive approach to landscape painting in Australia. His works often depicted the Australian bush, capturing the unique light, colors, and textures of the Australian landscape with a naturalistic and impressionistic style. Roberts' paintings are recognized for their authentic depiction of Australian scenery and their contribution to the development of Australian art.

Antonello da Messina was an Italian painter known for his skillful portrait painting and his pioneering use of oil painting techniques in Italy. His works often depicted religious subjects and portraits of prominent individuals, characterized by his meticulous attention to detail, realistic rendering of textures and expressions, and innovative use of light and shadow. Antonello's innovative use of oil painting techniques, such as the use of glazing and chiaroscuro, had a profound impact on the development of Italian Renaissance art and his works are recognized for their technical mastery and artistic sophistication.

Makoto Shinkai is a contemporary Japanese filmmaker known for his animated films and his unique approach to storytelling. His films, such as "Your Name" and "Weathering with You," are characterized by their breathtaking visuals, emotionally resonant narratives, and themes of love, loss, and human connections. Shinkai's films have earned him international acclaim for his innovative storytelling and artistic vision, making him one of the most influential figures in the field of animated film.

Hayao Miyazaki is a Japanese film director and co-founder of Studio Ghibli, known for his highly acclaimed animated films such as "My Neighbor Totoro," "Spirited Away," and "Princess Mononoke." His films are characterized by their enchanting storytelling, vibrant visuals, and ecological themes, often exploring the relationship between humanity and nature. Miyazaki's works have garnered international recognition and have had a profound impact on the world of animation and filmmaking.

Slim Aarons was an American photographer known for his iconic images of celebrities, socialites, and jet-setters during the mid-20th century. His works often captured the glamour and elegance of high society life, with a focus on fashion, travel, and leisure. Aarons' photographs are recognized for their refined compositions, vibrant colors, and candid moments, capturing the essence of the "good life" during that era.

Alfred Stevens was a 19th-century Belgian painter known for his realism and genre painting. His works often depicted everyday scenes of domestic life, interiors, and portraits, characterized by his meticulous attention to detail, skillful rendering of textures, and subtle use of light and shadow. Stevens' works are recognized for their naturalistic approach and emotional depth, providing glimpses into the ordinary lives of people during his time.

Albert Lynch was a Spanish painter known for his genre painting, particularly his depictions of elegant women in fashionable attire. His works often featured beautifully dressed women in luxurious settings, exuding a sense of elegance and sophistication. Lynch's paintings are recognized for their exquisite attention to detail, refined compositions, and skillful rendering of fabrics and textures.

Andre Kohn is a contemporary Russian-American painter known for his figurative art, often depicting dancers and musicians in dynamic poses. His works are characterized by their expressive brushwork, bold use of color, and emotional intensity, capturing the beauty and grace of the human form in motion. Kohn's paintings are recognized for their dynamic energy and passionate portrayal of the performing arts.

Daniel Garber was an American painter known for his landscape art, particularly his depictions of the Pennsylvania countryside. His works often portrayed serene and idyllic scenes of nature, characterized by his sensitive handling of light, atmospheric effects, and naturalistic details. Garber's landscape paintings are recognized for their tranquil and poetic quality, capturing the beauty and serenity of the American landscape.

Jacek Yerka is a contemporary Polish painter known for his surrealist artworks. His works often depict dreamlike and fantastical scenes, characterized by his meticulous attention to detail, imaginative compositions, and vibrant use of color. Yerka's paintings are recognized for their whimsical and thought-provoking nature, inviting viewers into a world of surreal imagination.

Beatrix Potter was a British writer and illustrator known for her beloved children's books, particularly the tales of Peter Rabbit and other animal characters. Her stories were often based on fairy tales and featured charming illustrations of anthropomorphic animals in pastoral settings. Potter's works are recognized for their timeless appeal, capturing the imaginations of generations of readers with their endearing characters and enchanting narratives.

René Magritte was a Belgian surrealist painter known for his enigmatic and thought-provoking artworks. His works often depicted ordinary objects and scenes in unconventional and surprising ways, challenging the viewers' perception of reality and the meaning of representation. Magritte's paintings are recognized for their clever use of symbolism, juxtaposition, and visual wit, inviting viewers to question the nature of reality and perception.

Georgia O'Keeffe was an American artist known for her contributions to abstract art and floral painting. Her works often depicted enlarged flowers, landscapes, and abstract forms, characterized by her bold use of color, simplified compositions, and strong sense of form.

O'Keeffe's paintings are recognized for their distinct style, which often combines abstraction and representation, creating a unique and mesmerizing visual experience.

Isaac Levitan was a Russian realist painter known for his depictions of the Russian landscape, particularly his atmospheric and poetic portrayals of forests, rivers, and meadows. His works often capture the fleeting moments of changing light and weather, evoking a sense of tranquility and contemplation. Levitan's paintings are recognized for their emotional depth, masterful handling of light and color, and profound connection to nature.

Frank Lloyd Wright was an American architect known for his innovative and influential designs that reshaped modern architecture. His works often featured organic forms, open floor plans, and seamless integration with the natural environment. Wright's architectural designs are recognized for their visionary approach, incorporating cutting-edge technologies and sustainable principles, and creating spaces that are harmonious with their surroundings.

Gustave Moreau was a French symbolist painter and sculptor known for his mythological and allegorical works. His paintings often depicted fantastical and otherworldly scenes, characterized by his intricate and detailed compositions, rich symbolism, and vivid use of color. Moreau's works are recognized for their mystical and enigmatic nature, exploring the depths of human emotions, spirituality, and imagination.

Ford Madox Brown was a British painter and a prominent member of the Pre-Raphaelite Brotherhood, a group of artists who sought to revive the artistic principles and techniques of early Italian Renaissance painters. His works often depicted historical and literary subjects, characterized by his meticulous attention to detail, vivid colors, and elaborate compositions. Brown's paintings are recognized for their meticulous craftsmanship, rich storytelling, and profound symbolism.

Ai Weiwei is a Chinese contemporary artist known for his conceptual art and installation art, often addressing social and political issues in China and around the world. His works are recognized for their thought-provoking nature, combining artistic expression with activism and advocating for human rights, freedom of speech, and social justice.

Tim Burton is an American film director, known for his distinctive style of gothic and macabre films. His works often feature fantastical and quirky elements, characterized by his unique visual aesthetic, dark humor, and unconventional storytelling. Burton's films, such as "Edward Scissorhands," "Beetlejuice," and "The Nightmare Before Christmas," have gained a cult following and have had a significant impact on contemporary popular culture.

Alfred Cheney Johnston was an American photographer known for his portraits of Ziegfeld Follies showgirls in the early 20th century. His works are recognized for their glamorous and sensual nature, capturing the beauty and allure of the performers through his masterful use of light, composition, and pose.

Duy Huynh is a Vietnamese American artist known for his whimsical and dreamlike paintings characterized by his use of bold colors, intricate patterns, and symbolic imagery. His works often explore themes of identity, spirituality, and the human condition, inviting viewers into a surreal and poetic world of imagination.

Michael Parkes is an American artist known for his stunning and detailed paintings that often blend elements of fantasy, mythology, and spirituality. His works are recognized for their meticulous craftsmanship, luminous colors, and otherworldly atmosphere, inviting viewers into a realm of magic and mystery.

Tintoretto, whose real name was Jacopo Comin, was an Italian painter of the Renaissance period known for his dynamic and dramatic compositions. His works often depicted religious and mythological subjects, characterized by his bold brushwork, vivid colors, and innovative use of light and shadow.

Archibald Thorburn was a Scottish painter known for his realistic depictions of birds and animals, particularly game birds and wildlife. His works are recognized for their meticulous attention to detail, exquisite rendering of feathers and fur, and naturalistic portrayal of the animals in their habitats.

Audrey Kawasaki is an American artist known for her unique style that combines elements of Japanese manga, Art Nouveau, and surrealism. Her works often depict young female figures with haunting expressions and intricate details, exploring themes of innocence, sensuality, and the complexities of human emotions.

George Lucas is an American film producer, director, and screenwriter, known for creating the "Star Wars" franchise, one of the most successful and influential film franchises in the history of cinema. His works have had a significant impact on popular culture, shaping the genre of speculative fiction film and inspiring generations of filmmakers and artists.

Arthur Streeton was an Australian landscape artist known for his impressionistic and plein air paintings of the Australian bush and coastal scenes. His works are recognized for their vibrant colors, loose brushwork, and evocative portrayal of the Australian landscape.

Albrecht Durer was a German painter, engraver, and printmaker known for his masterful works of mythological painting and landscape art during the Northern Renaissance. His works are recognized for their meticulous attention to detail, technical precision, and innovative use of perspective.

Andrea Kowch is an American painter known for her surreal and atmospheric landscapes that often depict solitary figures in dreamlike settings. Her works are recognized for their haunting beauty, evocative mood, and skillful handling of light and color.

Dorina Costras is a contemporary artist known for her abstract and expressive paintings characterized by her bold brushwork, vibrant colors, and emotional intensity. Her works often explore themes of identity, spirituality, and the human experience.

Alex Ross is an American comics artist known for his photorealistic and highly detailed artwork in the comic book industry. He is renowned for his iconic portrayals of superheroes and comic book characters, using traditional painting techniques to create stunning and dynamic illustrations that have earned him critical acclaim and a dedicated fan following.

Hasui Kawase was a Japanese printmaker and painter known for his shin-hanga style, which combined traditional Japanese woodblock print techniques with a modern sensibility. His works often depicted serene and picturesque landscapes of Japan, capturing the beauty of nature in a poetic and contemplative way.

Lucas Cranach the Elder was a German painter and printmaker known for his mythological paintings and portraits during the German Renaissance. His works are recognized for their rich colors, intricate details, and distinctive style, often featuring allegorical and mythological subjects that reflect the intellectual and artistic movements of his time.

Briton Rivière was an English painter known for his academic art and depictions of animals and wildlife. His works often depicted animals in a sentimental and anthropomorphic manner, reflecting his deep affinity and love for nature. His paintings are recognized for their technical skill, attention to detail, and emotional resonance.

Antonio Mora is a contemporary artist known for his mixed media artwork that combines photography with digital manipulation, creating surreal and evocative images. His works often explore themes of identity, memory, and the subconscious, inviting viewers into a world of mystery and introspection.

Mandy Disher is an artist known for her expressive and emotive paintings that often depict human figures in a raw and vulnerable state. Her works are recognized for their emotional depth, gestural brushwork, and powerful storytelling, capturing the complexities of the human experience with sensitivity and authenticity.

Henri-Edmond Cross was a French painter known for his involvement in the neo-impressionist movement, characterized by the use of broken color and optical effects in painting.

His works often depicted landscapes and seascapes with vibrant colors, capturing the play of light and color in nature with a sense of harmony and luminosity.

Auguste Toulmouche was a French painter known for his genre paintings, which depicted scenes from everyday life, often with a touch of elegance and romance. His works are recognized for their meticulous attention to detail, exquisite rendering of fabrics and textures, and skillful portrayal of human emotions.

Hubert Robert was a French painter known for his landscape art and his depictions of ruins and architectural scenes. His works often combined elements of romanticism and neoclassicism, capturing the beauty and serenity of nature, and the mystery and melancholy of ruins.

Syd Mead was an American designer and artist known for his work in the field of neo-futurism, particularly in the realm of conceptual design for science fiction films and video games. His works are recognized for their futuristic and visionary aesthetic, characterized by sleek and innovative designs that have influenced the look of many iconic science fiction films, such as "Blade Runner" and "Tron."

Carl Spitzweg was a German painter known for his post-romanticism style, which depicted everyday life and humorous scenes with a touch of whimsy and satire. His works are recognized for their delicate brushwork, intricate details, and witty storytelling, capturing the human condition with a sense of humor and irony.

Alyssa Monks is an American painter known for her exquisite and emotive portraits that often explore the complexities of human emotions and the fragility of human existence.

Her works are recognized for their meticulous attention to detail, luminous colors, and emotional depth, inviting viewers into an intimate and introspective world of the human psyche.

Edward Lear was an English artist and writer known for his landscape art and nonsense poetry. His works often depicted sweeping landscapes with a sense of grandeur and awe, capturing the beauty and majesty of nature. In addition to his landscape art, Lear is also known for his whimsical and humorous nonsense poetry, which often featured imaginative and nonsensical words and themes, showcasing his creative and playful spirit.

Ralph McQuarrie was an American artist known for his iconic concept artwork for the "Star Wars" film franchise. His imaginative and visionary designs helped shape the visual aesthetics of the "Star Wars" universe, including the look of characters, vehicles, and settings. His works are recognized for their stunning attention to detail, imaginative concepts, and ability to capture the essence of the "Star Wars" universe.

Sailor Moon is a Japanese anime and manga series created by Naoko Takeuchi. It is a popular and influential magical girl series that follows the adventures of a young girl named Usagi Tsukino, who transforms into the superhero Sailor Moon to protect the world from evil forces. Sailor Moon is known for its empowering themes of friendship, love, and self-acceptance, as well as its vibrant and colorful art style.

Simon Stålenhag is a Swedish artist known for his unique and evocative artwork that combines elements of science fiction, technology, and surrealism. His works often depict retrofuturistic landscapes and settings, showcasing a world where advanced technology and natural landscapes collide. Stålenhag's artwork is recognized for its atmospheric lighting, rich details, and thought-provoking storytelling, creating a sense of mystery and wonder.

Edward Robert Hughes was a British painter known for his romantic and ethereal paintings that often depicted fairy tale-like scenes and dreamy landscapes. His works are recognized for their exquisite use of light and color, creating a sense of otherworldliness and enchantment. Hughes' paintings often featured delicate and graceful figures, evoking a sense of beauty and mystery.

Jules Bastien-Lepage was a French painter known for his realistic and naturalistic style, often depicting rustic and rural scenes. He was associated with the artistic movement known as the "plein air" or outdoor painting, capturing the effects of light and atmosphere in his works with remarkable skill and sensitivity. Bastien-Lepage's paintings are recognized for their meticulous attention to detail, nuanced depictions of human emotions, and masterful use of color and light.

Richard S. Johnson was an American painter known for his impressionistic style and his vibrant and colorful landscapes. His works often depicted the beauty of nature in a loose and gestural manner, capturing the play of light and color with bold brushwork and a sense of spontaneity. Johnson's paintings are recognized for their dynamic compositions, expressive use of color, and emotional resonance, inviting viewers into a world of beauty and tranquility.

Rockwell Kent was an American painter known for his landscape art that often depicted the wilderness of Alaska and other remote regions. His works are recognized for their dramatic and majestic portrayal of nature, capturing the awe-inspiring beauty of the wilderness with a sense of grandeur and reverence. Kent's paintings often featured strong compositions, bold colors, and a sense of solitude and serenity.

Sparth, whose real name is Nicolas Bouvier, is a French artist and designer known for his futuristic and imaginative artwork. He is renowned for his concept designs for video games, films, and books, creating unique and otherworldly landscapes, cityscapes, and environments. Sparth's artwork is characterized by its futuristic and dystopian aesthetics, intricate details, and atmospheric lighting, creating a sense of awe and wonder.

Arnold Böcklin, Lovis Corinth, and Arnold Bocklin are renowned artists known for their contributions to landscape art and portraiture. Böcklin, a Swiss painter, was known for his mystical and fantastical landscapes that often depicted mythological and allegorical themes. Corinth, a German painter, was known for his bold and expressive brushwork in his landscape paintings and mythological works.

Robert Hagan, a naval officer turned artist, has gained recognition for his maritime-themed artworks, showcasing his deep understanding of ships and the ocean. Gregory Crewdson, a contemporary photographer, is known for his cinematic and atmospheric images that often blur the lines between reality and fiction, creating mysterious and thought-provoking narratives.

Thomas Benjamin Kennington, an English painter, is known for his genre paintings that often depicted working-class life and social issues of his time, showcasing his keen observation and empathy towards his subjects. Abbott Handerson Thayer, an American painter, was known for his landscape paintings that often displayed his exquisite sense of light, color, and atmosphere, capturing the beauty of nature in a poetic and evocative manner.

Gilbert Stuart, an American portrait painter, was renowned for his portraits of notable figures, including many U.S. presidents, capturing their likeness and character with his masterful technique and attention to detail. Louis Comfort Tiffany, an American artist and designer, was known for his contributions to the Art Nouveau movement, creating stained glass windows, lamps, and other decorative objects that showcased his innovative use of color, texture, and form.

Raphael Lacoste, a French artist and art director, is known for his visual storytelling through digital art and concept design, particularly in the field of video games and entertainment media. Jean Marc Nattier, a French painter, was known for his history paintings that often depicted mythological and allegorical themes with a focus on elegance and refinement in his compositions and color palette.

Janek Sedlar, a contemporary photographer, is known for his surreal and dreamlike images that often depict landscapes and nature in a fantastical and otherworldly manner. Sherree Valentine Daines, a British visual artist, is known for her expressive and colorful paintings, particularly in the genre of figurative art and portraiture.

Alexander Jansson, a Swedish illustrator, is known for his whimsical and imaginative illustrations that often depict fantastical worlds and characters, showcasing his unique storytelling and artistic style. James Turrell, an American artist, is known for his groundbreaking land art and light and space installations, creating immersive and transformative experiences through his use of light and space as artistic mediums.

Alex Grey, an American artist, is known for his figurative art that often combines spirituality, anatomy, and consciousness, creating thought-provoking and visionary artworks. Henri De Toulouse Lautrec, a French painter, was known for his genre paintings and animal paintings that often depicted the nightlife and social scenes of Paris, capturing the energy and spirit of the city in his vibrant and dynamic compositions.

Anton Pieck, a Dutch painter, was known for his nostalgic and charming paintings that often depicted scenes of the past, showcasing his meticulous attention to detail and his love for storytelling through his art. Ramon Casas, a Spanish impressionist painter, was known for his lively and colorful paintings that often depicted modern life and society, capturing the spirit of his time with his loose brushwork and bold use of color.

Andrew Atroshenko, a contemporary artist, is known for his romantic and poetic paintings that often depict intimate and emotional moments, showcasing his skillful use of light, color, and composition to create evocative and atmospheric artworks. Andy Kehoe, an American artist, is known for his surreal and imaginative paintings that often depict dreamlike and imaginary worlds, blending elements of fantasy, nature, and storytelling to create visually captivating narratives.

Andreas Achenbach, a German painter, was known for his landscape art, particularly his depictions of seascapes and coastal scenes. His works often captured the raw power and beauty of nature, showcasing his ability to convey the mood and atmosphere of the sea and its surroundings.

H.P. Lovecraft, an American author, is known for his influential contributions to the horror and science fiction genres. His works, including novels and short stories, are known for their vivid descriptions, rich imagination, and intricate mythologies, influencing many subsequent artists and writers.

Eric Zener, a contemporary painter, is known for his hyperrealistic artworks that often depict underwater scenes and swimmers, exploring themes of isolation, vulnerability, and the human connection with nature. His meticulous attention to detail and masterful use of light and color creates stunning and evocative paintings.

Kunisada, also known as Utagawa Kunisada, was a prominent ukiyo-e artist from the Utagawa school, which was one of the most well-known and prolific woodblock print schools in Japan during the Edo period. Kunisada's works often depicted scenes from Japanese history, kabuki theater, and daily life, showcasing his skill in capturing the intricacies of human expression and dramatic storytelling through his vibrant and detailed prints.

Quentin Tarantino, an American filmmaker, is known for his unique style of action films that often blend elements of pop culture, violence, and nonlinear storytelling. His films, such as Pulp Fiction, Reservoir Dogs, and Kill Bill, have gained a cult following and have been praised for their innovative storytelling, memorable characters, and dynamic action sequences. Tarantino has also made appearances as an actor in several of his own films and other productions.

Marianne North, a British landscape artist, was known for her botanical and floral paintings, particularly of exotic plants and landscapes from her travels around the world. Her works are characterized by their meticulous attention to detail, vibrant colors, and rich compositions, capturing the beauty and diversity of the natural world.

Vivienne Westwood, a British fashion designer, is known for her influential contributions to the punk counterculture and her avant-garde designs that challenge traditional notions of fashion and gender. She has been a prominent figure in the fashion industry for decades, known for her edgy and rebellious designs that push the boundaries of style and social norms.

Cindy Sherman, an American artist, is known for her thought-provoking and feminist artworks, particularly her self-portraits that challenge notions of identity, gender, and representation. Sherman often transforms herself into various characters and personas, using costumes, props, and photography to create powerful and provocative images that challenge societal norms and expectations.

Scott Listfield is a contemporary American artist known for his unique style of blending science fiction and pop culture references in his paintings. His works often depict lone astronauts exploring dystopian and post-apocalyptic landscapes, creating a sense of isolation and wonder. Listfield's paintings are characterized by their meticulous attention to detail, atmospheric lighting, and thought-provoking narratives that explore themes of technology, humanity, and the future.

Alexandre Cabanel was a 19th-century French painter known for his genre paintings and academic art style. He was a prominent figure in the French academic art scene, known for his polished and idealized depictions of mythological and historical subjects. Cabanel's works are characterized by their technical skill, attention to detail, and refined compositions, often featuring sensuous figures and lush landscapes.

Arthur Rackham was a British illustrator known for his whimsical and fantastical illustrations, particularly in fairy tale and children's book illustrations. His intricate and imaginative artworks often featured magical creatures, enchanted forests, and otherworldly scenes, capturing the imagination of generations of readers. Rackham's illustrations are characterized by their intricate linework, delicate color palettes, and attention to detail, creating a sense of wonder and enchantment in his works.

Arthur Hacker was a British painter known for his portraits and genre paintings. His works often depicted idealized and romanticized scenes from history and mythology, showcasing his skill in capturing the human form and expression. Hacker's paintings are characterized by their classical influences, soft and glowing lighting, and richly detailed compositions.

Henri Fantin-Latour was a French painter known for his realist works and mythological paintings. He was a prominent figure in the 19th-century French art scene, known for his meticulous attention to detail and skillful rendering of textures and surfaces. Fantin-Latour's works often featured intimate and introspective portraits, allegorical and mythological scenes, and still life compositions, capturing the beauty and essence of his subjects with a sense of quiet contemplation.

Mark Ryden is a contemporary American painter known for his surrealist and pop-surrealist artworks. His works often feature a mix of innocent and eerie imagery, blending elements of popular culture, vintage aesthetics, and dark symbolism. Ryden's paintings are characterized by their meticulous details, rich symbolism, and thought-provoking narratives that explore themes of childhood, innocence, and the human condition.

Peter Holme III is an artist known for his unique style of blending traditional oil painting techniques with modern subject matter. His works often feature surreal and dreamlike compositions, showcasing his skill in capturing light, color, and texture in his oil paintings. Holme's artworks are characterized by their otherworldly and fantastical elements, creating a sense of wonder and intrigue in his works.

Ted Nasmith is a Canadian artist known for his illustrations of fantasy literature, particularly J.R.R. Tolkien's works, including The Lord of the Rings and The Silmarillion. His highly detailed and atmospheric illustrations bring Tolkien's fantastical world to life, capturing the landscapes, characters, and epic battles of Middle-earth with a sense of grandeur and beauty.

Bill Gekas is an Australian photographer known for his unique and nostalgic portraits of his daughter, often inspired by classical paintings and historical art styles. His works are characterized by their impeccable attention to detail, lighting, and composition, capturing the essence of his subjects with a timeless and nostalgic quality.

Paul Strand was an American photographer known for his pioneering contributions to modern photography in the early 20th century. His works often featured stark and minimalist compositions, showcasing his mastery of form, tone, and contrast. Strand's photographs are characterized by their poetic and evocative qualities, capturing the beauty and simplicity of everyday life with a sense of intimacy and depth.

Anne Stokes is a British artist and illustrator known for her fantasy and gothic-themed artworks. Her works often feature mystical creatures, mythical beings, and dark fantasy settings, showcasing her skill in creating detailed and imaginative worlds. Stokes' artworks are characterized by their intricate linework, rich color palettes, and atmospheric lighting, creating a sense of mystery and enchantment in her works.

David Teniers the Younger was a 17th-century Flemish painter known for his mythological paintings and landscape art. He was a prominent figure in the Baroque art movement, known for his skillful rendering of landscapes, genre scenes, and mythological narratives. Teniers' works are characterized by their vibrant color palettes, dynamic compositions, and richly detailed depictions of everyday life and fantastical worlds.

Alan Lee is a British painter and illustrator known for his work on fantasy literature, particularly his illustrations for J.R.R. Tolkien's works, including The Lord of the Rings and The Hobbit. His detailed and evocative artworks bring Tolkien's imaginary world to life, capturing the landscapes, characters, and epic battles with a sense of wonder and authenticity. Lee's illustrations are characterized by their meticulous attention to detail, rich color palettes, and atmospheric lighting, creating a sense of immersion in his works.

Ed Freeman is a helicopter pilot and artist known for his aerial paintings of landscapes and natural scenery. His unique perspective from the cockpit of his helicopter allows him to capture breathtaking and panoramic views of the world from above. Freeman's artworks are characterized by their sweeping vistas, vibrant color palettes, and dynamic compositions, showcasing the beauty and majesty of the natural world.

Andrey Remnev is a contemporary Russian artist known for his iconography, a traditional form of religious art in Eastern Orthodox Christianity. His works often depict religious figures, biblical scenes, and spiritual symbolism, capturing the spiritual essence and reverence of Orthodox iconography with his meticulous attention to detail and masterful use of color and composition. Remnev's artworks are characterized by their spiritual depth, symbolic richness, and classical techniques, creating a sense of awe and reverence in his works.

Alasdair McLellan is a contemporary British photographer known for his fashion and portrait photography. His works often feature intimate and candid portraits of models, celebrities, and everyday people, capturing their personalities, emotions, and unique beauty. McLellan's photographs are characterized by their raw and authentic quality, often showcasing a sense of vulnerability and intimacy in his subjects, and his use of lighting and composition to create striking visual narratives.

Botero, whose full name is Fernando Botero, is a Colombian figurative artist known for his distinctive style of depicting voluptuous and rotund figures in his artworks. His works often explore themes of political satire, social commentary, and allegory, using his unique and exaggerated figures to create provocative and thought-provoking narratives. Botero's artworks are characterized by their bold and exaggerated forms, vibrant color palettes, and a sense of humor and satire in his depictions of human figures and society.

Vittorio Matteo Corcos was an Italian portrait painter known for his genre paintings and depictions of high society in the late 19th and early 20th centuries. His works often featured elegant and refined scenes of fashionable people in luxurious settings, capturing the glamour, elegance, and sophistication of his subjects. Corcos' paintings are characterized by their meticulous attention to detail, rich color palettes, and exquisite rendering of fabrics, textures, and facial expressions.

Ed Mell is a contemporary American painter known for his bold and vibrant depictions of the American Southwest landscape. His works often feature dramatic rock formations, vast desert vistas, and the unique light and colors of the Southwest. Mell's paintings are characterized by their dynamic compositions, expressive brushwork, and rich color palettes, capturing the beauty and ruggedness of the Southwest landscape.

Worthington Whittredge was a 19th-century American landscape painter known for his realistic and atmospheric depictions of the American wilderness. His works often portrayed serene and idyllic scenes of forests, rivers, and mountains, capturing the tranquility and grandeur of the American landscape. Whittredge's paintings are characterized by their meticulous attention to detail, naturalistic color palettes, and a sense of reverence for nature.

Jakub Różalski is a contemporary Polish illustrator known for his imaginative and evocative artworks, often featuring dystopian and fantastical themes. His works often depict hauntingly beautiful landscapes, mysterious characters, and imaginative creatures, creating a sense of otherworldliness in his illustrations. Różalski's artworks are characterized by their intricate details, atmospheric lighting, and a sense of narrative storytelling.

Alex Gross is a contemporary American painter known for his surreal and thought-provoking artworks. His works often combine elements of pop culture, historical references, and dreamlike imagery, creating unique and compelling visual narratives. Gross' paintings are characterized by their meticulous rendering, juxtaposition of contrasting elements, and a sense of mystery and intrigue in his compositions.

Edward Weston was a 20th-century American photographer known for his pioneering work in modernist photography, particularly his landscapes, still lifes, and portraits. His works often focused on the ordinary and overlooked objects and scenes, capturing their inherent beauty through his mastery of composition, lighting, and form. Weston's photographs are characterized by their precise compositions, rich tonal ranges, and a sense of abstraction and visual poetry.

Ilya Kuvshinov is a contemporary Russian artist known for his digital illustrations, particularly his character designs and portraits. His works often feature stunningly detailed and beautifully rendered characters, capturing their personalities, emotions, and unique aesthetics. Kuvshinov's artworks are characterized by their vibrant color palettes, dynamic compositions, and a sense of elegance and grace in his depictions.

Francisco de Goya was an 18th-century Spanish painter known for his diverse body of work, including mythological paintings, portraits, and social commentary. His mythological paintings often depicted dramatic and powerful scenes from Greek and Roman mythology, showcasing his skill in capturing the human form and emotions. Goya's paintings are characterized by their emotional intensity, dramatic lighting, and a sense of darkness and ambiguity in his compositions, reflecting the romanticism of his time.

Balthus, whose full name is Balthasar Klossowski, was a 20th-century French painter known for his enigmatic and provocative artworks. His landscape paintings often featured dreamlike and surreal elements, creating mysterious and unsettling visual narratives. Balthus' paintings are characterized by their meticulous attention to detail, symbolic imagery, and a sense of tension and ambiguity in his compositions, reflecting his unique style of surrealism.

J.C. Leyendecker was an American illustrator known for his iconic depictions of idealized American life, particularly in his advertisements and magazine covers. His works often portrayed handsome men, beautiful women, and idyllic domestic scenes, capturing the optimism and aspirations of the American Dream. Leyendecker's illustrations are characterized by their bold and dynamic compositions, vibrant color palettes, and a sense of elegance and glamour in his depictions.

Nathan Wirth is a contemporary American photographer known for his captivating and moody landscapes. His works often feature dramatic and atmospheric scenes, capturing the beauty and mystery of the natural world. Wirth's photographs are characterized by their use of light and shadow, evocative tones, and a sense of solitude and introspection in his compositions, creating a poetic and emotional connection with the landscapes he captures.

Albert Goodwin was a 19th-century English painter known for his landscape paintings, particularly his depictions of remote and exotic locations. His works often portrayed serene and atmospheric scenes of landscapes, seascapes, and cityscapes, capturing the beauty and grandeur of the natural world. Goodwin's paintings are characterized by their meticulous attention to detail, luminous color palettes, and a sense of adventure and exploration in his compositions.

Ferdinand Hodler was a Swiss symbolist painter known for his powerful and emotionally charged artworks. His works often depicted allegorical and mythological themes, exploring the depths of human emotions and spirituality. Hodler's paintings are characterized by their bold and expressive brushwork, rich color palettes, and a sense of symbolism and allegory in his compositions, reflecting his unique style of symbolism.

Charles Spencelayh was a British genre painter known for his meticulous and highly detailed depictions of everyday life. His works often portrayed scenes of ordinary people engaged in simple tasks, capturing the charm and humor of everyday situations. Spencelayh's paintings are characterized by their precise rendering, naturalistic color palettes, and a sense of warmth and nostalgia in his compositions, reflecting his keen observation of human behavior and his love for genre painting.

Louise Dahl-Wolfe was an American photographer known for her pioneering work in fashion and portrait photography. Her photographs often featured elegant and stylish models in glamorous settings, capturing the beauty and sophistication of fashion and culture. Dahl-Wolfe's photographs are characterized by their exquisite compositions, use of natural light, and a sense of elegance and timelessness in her depictions, setting new standards for fashion photography in her time.

Amy Judd is a contemporary British artist known for her intricate and surreal artworks, often depicting mysterious and ethereal female figures. Her works often combine elements of fantasy, nature, and symbolism, creating dreamlike and poetic visual narratives. Judd's artworks are characterized by their delicate and detailed rendering, muted color palettes, and a sense of otherworldliness and mystery in her compositions.

Kitagawa Utamaro was an 18th-century Japanese artist known for his ukiyo-e prints, particularly his depictions of beautiful women. His works often portrayed graceful and sensuous female figures in various settings, capturing the elegance and charm of the floating world. Utamaro's prints are characterized by their exquisite details, vibrant color palettes, and a sense of refinement and sophistication in his compositions, making him one of the most renowned ukiyo-e artists of his time.

Igor Zenin is a contemporary Russian artist known for his unique and imaginative artworks, often combining elements of surrealism, fantasy, and science fiction. His works often feature fantastical creatures, futuristic landscapes, and otherworldly environments, creating intriguing and visually stunning visual narratives. Zenin's artworks are characterized by their bold and imaginative compositions, vibrant color palettes, and a sense of wonder and mystery in his depictions.

Carlo Crivelli was a 15th-century Italian painter known for his intricate and highly detailed paintings, particularly his depictions of religious subjects. His works often featured richly

ornamented and fantastical settings, capturing the intricate details and symbolic meanings of religious narratives. Crivelli's
paintings are characterized by their meticulous rendering, lavish use of gold leaf, and a sense of mysticism and spirituality in
his compositions, reflecting the artistic style of the Gothic era.

Edmund Leighton was a 19th-century British painter
known for his genre paintings, particularly his depictions of
medieval and romantic scenes. His works often portrayed
chivalry, romance, and courtly love, capturing the idealized vision of the Middle Ages. Leighton's paintings are characterized
by their meticulous attention to detail, rich color palettes, and
a sense of narrative and storytelling in his compositions, reflecting his adherence to the ideals of the Pre-Raphaelite
Brotherhood, a group of artists who sought to revive the aesthetics of the early Renaissance.

Bjarke Ingels is a contemporary Danish architect known
for his innovative and visionary designs. His works often challenge traditional architectural conventions, incorporating sustainable and environmental considerations, and pushing the
boundaries of form and function. Ingels' architectural designs
are characterized by their bold and futuristic aesthetics, harmonious integration with the natural environment, and a sense
of playfulness and creativity in his compositions, reflecting his
commitment to creating architecture that is both functional
and inspiring.

Diego Velázquez was a 17th-century Spanish painter
known for his masterful technique and innovative compositions. His works often depicted a wide range of subjects, including mythological scenes, historical events, and portraits.
Velázquez's paintings are characterized by their naturalistic ap-

proach, use of light and shadow, and a sense of psychological depth in his depictions, reflecting his ability to capture the inner emotions and personalities of his subjects. His mythological paintings often portrayed classical themes with a sense of realism and humanity, setting him apart from his contemporaries.

Bernardo Bellotto was an 18th-century Italian painter known for his cityscape and landscape paintings. His works often depicted urban scenes, capturing the architectural splendor and atmospheric charm of cities in Europe. Bellotto's paintings are characterized by their meticulous attention to detail, accurate perspective, and a sense of depth and realism in his compositions. His landscape paintings often portrayed natural settings with a sense of serenity and harmony, capturing the beauty of the natural world in a timeless manner.

John Singleton Copley was an 18th-century American painter known for his portraits and historical paintings. His works often portrayed prominent figures of his time, including politicians, military leaders, and members of high society. Copley's portraits are characterized by their meticulous attention to detail, lifelike depictions of his subjects, and a sense of dignity and elegance in his compositions. His historical paintings often portrayed significant events of American history, capturing the drama and emotion of those moments with a sense of realism and narrative storytelling.

Horace Vernet was a 19th-century French painter known for his landscape paintings, particularly his depictions of military scenes and romanticized landscapes. His works often portrayed war scenes, battles, and soldiers, capturing the heroism and drama of military life. Vernet's paintings are characterized by their dramatic compositions, dynamic brushwork, and a sense of action and movement in his depictions. His romanticized landscapes often portrayed exotic locations with a sense of adventure and exploration, reflecting the spirit of Romanticism in his art.

Hiroshi Yoshida was a 20th-century Japanese artist known for his woodblock prints, particularly his depictions of landscapes and nature. His works often portrayed serene and contemplative scenes of mountains, rivers, and forests, capturing the beauty and tranquility of the Japanese landscape. Yoshida's prints are characterized by their delicate and intricate details, vibrant color palettes, and a sense of harmony and balance in his compositions. His prints often incorporated Western techniques and aesthetics, blending traditional Japanese art with modern influences.

Walter Crane was a 19th-century British painter and illustrator known for his symbolist artworks and contributions to the Arts and Crafts movement. His works often depicted allegorical and mythological themes, exploring the social and political issues of his time. Crane's paintings are characterized by their intricate and decorative details, rich color palettes, and a sense of symbolism and allegory in his compositions. His artworks often carried a moral or social message, advocating for social reform, women's rights, and other progressive causes of his time. Crane's illustrations were widely used in books, magazines, and other publications, and his artistic style had a significant impact on the aesthetics of the Arts and Crafts movement, which emphasized the integration of art and craftsmanship in everyday life.

Anka Zhuravleva is a contemporary Russian artist known for her surreal and dreamlike artworks. Her works often depict fantastical and otherworldly scenes, blurring the lines between reality and imagination. Zhuravleva's paintings are characterized by their meticulous attention to detail, unique visual narratives, and a sense of mystery and enchantment in her compositions. Her artworks often evoke a sense of wonder and intrigue, inviting viewers to explore the depths of their own imagination.

Robert McGinnis is a contemporary American painter and illustrator known for his iconic artworks, particularly his depictions of women in popular culture. His works often portray glamorous and sultry women, capturing the beauty and allure of the female form. McGinnis' paintings are characterized by their bold and dynamic compositions, vibrant color palettes, and a sense of sensuality and elegance in his depictions. His illustrations have been widely used in book covers, movie posters, and other forms of media, becoming iconic representations of the feminine mystique.

John Wilhelm is a contemporary Swiss photographer known for his imaginative and humorous digital artworks. His works often combine photography with digital manipulation, creating whimsical and surreal scenes that defy reality. Wilhelm's photographs are characterized by their creativity, attention to detail, and a sense of playfulness in his compositions. His artworks often blend elements of fantasy, surrealism, and humor, inviting viewers to enter into his imaginative world and see ordinary objects and scenes in a new and unexpected light.

Anna Dittmann is a contemporary American artist known for her ethereal and fantastical artworks. Her works often depict dreamlike and otherworldly scenes, featuring mystical creatures, haunting landscapes, and intricate details. Dittmann's paintings are characterized by their delicate and intricate brushwork, rich color palettes, and a sense of enchantment and mystery in her compositions. Her artworks often evoke a sense of wonder and evoke emotions, inviting viewers to immerse themselves in her mystical and imaginative world.

Bo Bartlett is a contemporary American painter known for his realist artworks that capture the essence of American life and culture. His works often depict ordinary scenes and people, capturing the beauty and complexity of everyday life. Bartlett's paintings are characterized by their meticulous attention to detail, luminous color palettes, and a sense of nostalgia and reverence in his compositions. His artworks often evoke a sense of timelessness and emotional depth, inviting viewers to reflect on the human condition and the beauty of the world around us.

Michal Karcz is a contemporary Polish artist known for his surreal and atmospheric digital artworks. His works often depict otherworldly landscapes and dreamlike scenes, blending elements of fantasy, science fiction, and surrealism. Karcz's digital paintings are characterized by their rich and moody color palettes, intricate details, and a sense of mystery and wonder in his compositions. His artworks often evoke a sense of escapism, inviting viewers to immerse themselves in his imaginative and captivating world.

Mort Kunstler is a contemporary American painter known for his historical artworks, particularly his depictions of American Civil War scenes. His paintings often portray key moments and figures from the Civil War era, capturing the drama, emotion, and intensity of this pivotal period in American history. Kunstler's artworks are characterized by their meticulous attention to historical accuracy, vivid storytelling, and a sense of patriotism in his compositions. His paintings have been widely exhibited and collected, earning him recognition as one of the foremost painters of Civil War art.

Adrianus Eversen was a 19th-century Dutch painter known for his meticulously detailed and atmospheric cityscape paintings. His works often depicted scenes from everyday life in the streets of Dutch towns and cities, capturing the charm and character of urban landscapes during the 19th century. Eversen's paintings are characterized by their intricate architectural details, subtle play of light and shadow, and a sense of nostalgia in his compositions. His artworks are considered important representations of Dutch 19th-century cityscapes and continue to be admired for their technical skill and artistic vision.

Brad Kunkle is a contemporary American artist known for his luminous and ethereal paintings that blend traditional oil painting techniques with modern elements. His works often depict women in otherworldly and fantastical settings, exploring themes of femininity, spirituality, and the natural world. Kunkle's paintings are characterized by their exquisite attention to detail, delicate use of color and light, and a sense of mystery and allure in his compositions. His artworks have been exhibited and collected internationally, gaining him recognition as a leading artist in the contemporary figurative art movement.

Bella Kotak is a contemporary British photographer known for her enchanting and whimsical portraits that capture the beauty of nature and femininity. Her works often depict women in dreamlike and magical settings, using elaborate costumes, props, and natural landscapes to create stunning visual narratives. Kotak's photographs are characterized by their meticulous attention to detail, soft and muted color palettes, and a sense of wonder and escapism in her compositions. Her artworks have gained her a large following on social media and have been featured in numerous exhibitions and publications.

Paul Delvaux was a Belgian surrealist painter known for his enigmatic and evocative artworks. His works often depicted dreamlike and mysterious scenes, featuring strange juxtapositions of objects and figures in surreal landscapes. Delvaux's paintings are characterized by their precise and meticulous brushwork, muted color palettes, and a sense of unease and tension in his compositions. His artworks often explore themes of desire, isolation, and the human subconscious, inviting viewers to interpret and interpret his enigmatic visual narratives.

Victo Ngai is a contemporary Chinese illustrator known for her intricate and fantastical artworks. Her works often blend elements of mythology, fantasy, and storytelling, creating rich and immersive visual narratives. Ngai's illustrations are characterized by their intricate details, bold and vibrant color palettes, and a sense of wonder and magic in her compositions.

Her artworks have been widely used in books, magazines, and other forms of media, earning her recognition as one of the leading illustrators in the industry.

Abbott Fuller Graves was an American painter known for his realism and genre paintings. His works often depicted scenes from everyday life, capturing the charm and character of rural and urban landscapes, as well as intimate domestic scenes. Graves' paintings are characterized by their attention to detail, skillful rendering of light and shadow, and a sense of warmth and humanity in his compositions. His artworks often portray ordinary moments and people with a sense of nostalgia and sentimentality, inviting viewers to connect with the human experience depicted in his works.

Patrice Murciano is a contemporary French artist known for his vibrant and dynamic artworks that blend abstract and figurative elements. His works often feature bold and expressive brushwork, vibrant color palettes, and a sense of movement and energy in his compositions. Murciano's artworks are characterized by their bold and expressive style, capturing the essence of his subjects in a unique and captivating way. His paintings have been exhibited internationally and collected by art enthusiasts worldwide.

Alexandre Calame was a 19th-century Swiss painter known for his landscape art and his contributions to the Romantic movement. His works often depicted grand and majestic landscapes, including mountains, forests, and lakes, capturing the awe-inspiring beauty of nature. Calame's paintings are characterized by their dramatic use of light and shadow, meticulous attention to detail, and a sense of awe and wonder in his compositions. His artworks were highly regarded during his time and continue to be admired for their technical skill and artistic vision.

Bob Byerley was an American painter known for his nostalgic and heartwarming artworks that capture the innocence of childhood and the charm of small-town America. His works often depict scenes of children engaged in play, surrounded by vintage toys, and set against the backdrop of idyllic American landscapes. Byerley's paintings are characterized by their nostalgic and sentimental style, with a focus on storytelling and capturing the essence of a bygone era. His artworks have been widely collected and appreciated for their nostalgic appeal and emotional resonance.

Cicely Mary Barker was a British painter and illustrator known for her enchanting and delicate artworks featuring fairies and flowers. Her works often depicted fairies in natural settings, surrounded by flowers and plants, capturing the beauty and magic of the natural world. Barker's illustrations are characterized by their exquisite attention to detail, soft and muted color palettes, and a sense of innocence and wonder in her compositions. Her artworks have been widely loved and cherished by generations of readers, earning her recognition as one of the foremost artists in the genre of fairy art.

Kadir Nelson is a contemporary American artist and graphic designer known for his powerful and emotive artworks that celebrate African-American culture and history. His works often depict African-American figures, including historical icons, everyday people, and children, capturing their strength, resilience, and beauty. Nelson's artworks are characterized by their vibrant color palettes, rich textures, and a sense of pride and dignity in his subjects. His illustrations have been featured in numerous books, magazines, and other forms of media, earning him widespread acclaim and recognition for his artistic talent and impactful storytelling.

Kengo Kuma is a contemporary Japanese architect known for his innovative and sustainable architectural designs that blend traditional Japanese aesthetics with modern technology and materials. His works often incorporate natural elements, such as wood, stone, and light, to create harmonious and organic spaces that are deeply rooted in their surrounding environments. Kuma's architectural designs are characterized by their minimalist and elegant style, attention to detail, and a sense of balance and harmony in his compositions. His buildings have been internationally recognized for their unique and thoughtful approach to architecture and their contribution to sustainable design.

The Brothers Grimm were 19th-century German authors and cultural researchers known for their collection of fairy tales, which have become some of the most beloved and widely known stories in the world. Their collection, often referred to as Grimm's Fairy Tales, includes over 200 stories, such as Cinderella, Snow White, Hansel and Gretel, Little Red Riding Hood, and many more. The Brothers Grimm's fairy tales are characterized by their rich storytelling, memorable characters, and timeless themes of morality, courage, and the power of imagination. Their works have been translated into numerous languages and have inspired countless adaptations in literature, theater, film, and other forms of media, making them an enduring and influential part of global folklore and literary heritage.

Jovana Rikalo is a contemporary fine art photographer known for her ethereal and dreamlike images that capture the beauty and mystery of the natural world. Her works often feature female figures in poetic and introspective poses, surrounded by nature, evoking a sense of enchantment and wonder. Rikalo's photographs are characterized by their soft and muted color palettes, delicate compositions, and a sense of other-worldliness in her imagery. Her artworks have been exhibited internationally and have garnered acclaim for their evocative and emotive storytelling.

Malcolm Liepke is a contemporary American painter known for his expressive and gestural figurative artworks that capture the human form with dynamic brushwork and bold color choices. His works often depict intimate and introspective moments, capturing the emotions and vulnerabilities of his subjects. Liepke's paintings are characterized by their loose and painterly style, capturing the essence of the human form with a sense of movement and energy. His artworks have been exhibited in galleries and museums worldwide and have earned him recognition as one of the foremost contemporary figurative painters.

Bert Stern was an American photographer known for his iconic images of celebrities, fashion, and advertising. He was known for his distinctive style, which often featured bold compositions, vibrant colors, and a sense of glamour and sophistication. Stern's photographs ranged from fashion editorials to celebrity portraits, and his subjects included Marilyn Monroe, Audrey Hepburn, Elizabeth Taylor, and many other famous personalities. His photographs have been widely published in magazines, exhibited in galleries, and collected by art collectors and enthusiasts for their iconic and enduring appeal.

Alice Neel was an American painter known for her portraits, cityscapes, and landscape artworks that captured the essence of her subjects and surroundings with raw and emotive brushwork. Her works often depicted everyday people, including friends, family, and strangers, with a sense of humanity and empathy. Neel's paintings are characterized by their bold and expressive style, capturing the psychological and emotional aspects of her subjects with a sense of intimacy and vulnerability. Her artworks have been exhibited in museums and galleries internationally and have earned her recognition as one of the foremost portrait painters of the 20th century.

Moebius, also known as Jean Giraud, was a French artist and writer known for his influential contributions to western films and comics. He was known for his distinctive style, which blended science fiction, fantasy, and surrealism, creating intricate and otherworldly worlds that captured the imagination of readers and viewers alike. Moebius' artworks are characterized by their detailed and imaginative compositions, intricate linework, and a sense of mysticism and wonder in his storytelling. His works have been widely published and have influenced numerous artists and filmmakers, earning him a reputation as a visionary in the field of comics and illustration.

Alex Colville was a Canadian painter known for his realist artworks that depicted everyday life and ordinary moments with a sense of mystery and tension. His works often featured figures in everyday settings, capturing their emotions and psychological states with precision and depth. Colville's paintings are characterized by their meticulous attention to detail, muted color palettes, and a sense of quiet introspection in his compositions. His artworks have been exhibited in museums and galleries worldwide and have earned him recognition as one of Canada's most prominent painters.

Andreas Franke is a contemporary Austrian photographer known for his innovative underwater photographic installations that blend photography and surreal elements. Franke's works often feature underwater scenes that are combined with manipulated or staged photographs, creating a unique and captivating visual experience. His installations are characterized by their intricate details, imaginative storytelling, and a sense of mystique and enigma. Franke's artworks have been exhibited internationally and have received critical acclaim for their innovative approach to blending photography and surreal elements in an underwater setting.

Gjon Mili was an Albanian-American photographer known for his pioneering work in the field of stroboscopic photography, which involved using multiple flashlights to capture motion and create dynamic and energetic images. Mili's works often featured dancers, athletes, and other subjects in motion, capturing their movements with a sense of grace and fluidity. His photographs are characterized by their innovative use of light and motion, creating a sense of dynamism and energy in his images. Mili's works have been widely published and exhibited, earning him recognition as one of the pioneers of stroboscopic photography.

Arthur Wardle was a British painter known for his detailed and realistic artworks that depicted animals, especially dogs and horses, in naturalistic and often sentimental settings. Wardle's works often featured animals in pastoral or hunting scenes, capturing their beauty, strength, and elegance with meticulous brushwork and attention to detail. His paintings are characterized by their rich color palettes, realistic depictions of fur and feathers, and a sense of intimacy and connection with the animal subjects. Wardle's artworks have been exhibited in galleries and museums, and his depictions of animals have earned him recognition as one of the prominent animal painters of his time.

Alan Bean was an American astronaut and painter known for his unique artworks that depicted the experiences and landscapes of the moon, as he was the fourth person to walk on the moon during the Apollo 12 mission in 1969. Bean's paintings captured the lunar surface, moonwalks, and other celestial scenes with a sense of wonder and awe, based on his firsthand experiences as an astronaut. His artworks are characterized by their detailed and realistic depictions of lunar landscapes, combined with his artistic interpretation of the moon's beauty and mysteries. Bean's paintings have been exhibited in museums and galleries and are considered important artistic representations of the moon landings and space exploration.

Ernst Ludwig Kirchner was a German painter and printmaker known for his expressionist artworks that depicted landscapes, genre scenes, and the human figure with bold and vibrant colors, energetic brushwork, and emotional intensity. Kirchner's works often reflected his inner struggles, as well as his observations of society and the human condition. His paintings are characterized by their distorted perspectives, bold color palettes, and expressive forms, capturing the essence of his subjects with a sense of rawness and emotional depth.

Kirchner's artworks have been exhibited internationally and are considered important contributions to the expressionist movement in art.

Kevin Sloan is a contemporary American painter known for his imaginative and thought-provoking artworks that blend elements of surrealism, symbolism, and narrative storytelling. Sloan's works often feature dreamlike and fantastical scenes, depicting animals, objects, and human figures in unusual and unexpected settings, inviting viewers to interpret and interpret their meaning. His paintings are characterized by their meticulous attention to detail, symbolic imagery, and a sense of mystery and intrigue in his narratives. Sloan's artworks have been exhibited in galleries and museums and have earned him recognition as a prominent contemporary surrealist painter.

Miho Hirano is a contemporary Japanese painter known for her ethereal and enchanting artworks that depict female figures in dreamlike and fantastical settings, often surrounded by flora and fauna. Hirano's works are characterized by their delicate and intricate details, soft color palettes, and a sense of otherworldliness in her compositions. Her paintings often convey a sense of beauty, fragility, and serenity, capturing the essence of femininity and nature in a surreal and poetic way. Hirano's artworks have been exhibited in galleries and art shows internationally and have gained a significant following for their unique and captivating style.

Russ Mills, also known as Byroglyphics, is a contemporary British artist known for his dynamic and expressive artworks that combine elements of traditional and digital media. Mills' works often feature portraits and figures rendered in a mix of collage, drawing, and painting techniques, resulting in visually striking and emotionally charged images. His artworks are characterized by their bold and energetic brushwork, intricate detailing, and a sense of raw emotion and intensity. Mills' works have been exhibited in galleries and art shows worldwide and have earned him recognition as a leading contemporary artist.

Boris Kustodiev was a Russian painter known for his genre art and portraits that depicted the life and culture of Russia in the early 20th century. Kustodiev's works often featured scenes of rural life, traditional festivals, and everyday activities of the Russian people, capturing the essence of Russian culture, traditions, and customs. His paintings are characterized by their rich and vibrant color palettes, intricate detailing, and a sense of nostalgia and romanticism in his portrayal of the Russian way of life. Kustodiev's artworks have been exhibited in museums and galleries in Russia and internationally, and he is considered one of the prominent painters of the Russian artistic tradition.

Andrea Mantegna was an Italian painter known for his mythological paintings and allegorical works. He was a prominent figure of the Renaissance period and his works often depicted classical themes and subjects. Mantegna's paintings were characterized by their meticulous attention to detail, use of perspective, and dramatic compositions that conveyed a sense of grandeur and monumentality.

Hsiao-Ron Cheng is a contemporary Taiwanese artist known for her unique and dreamlike artworks. Her works often feature ethereal and surreal depictions of young women in serene and otherworldly settings. Cheng's artworks are characterized by their soft color palettes, delicate brushwork, and a sense of tranquility and introspection.

Carl Holsoe was a Danish painter known for his intimate interior scenes and quiet depictions of everyday life. His works often portrayed serene and peaceful interiors with muted color palettes, capturing the subtle play of light and shadow in domestic settings. Holsoe's paintings were characterized by their attention to detail, realistic rendering, and a sense of tranquility and solitude.

Jeff Goldblum is an American actor known for his roles in western films and television shows. He has appeared in various western-themed films and TV shows, portraying characters with distinctive personalities and mannerisms. Goldblum is known for his versatile acting skills and his ability to bring depth and complexity to his roles, including his performances in western-themed productions.

Tadao Ando is a Japanese architect known for his minimalist and modernist designs. He has designed numerous buildings around the world, including museums, churches, and residential structures. Ando's works are characterized by their simple and clean lines, use of natural light, and integration of architecture with the surrounding environment.

Tibor Nagy is a researcher known for his contributions in a specific field or area of expertise, although the specific field or area of research is not mentioned in the prompt.

Charles-Francois Daubigny was a French painter known for his landscape art and his role in the Barbizon school, a group of artists who painted en plein air and depicted natural landscapes in a realistic and naturalistic style. Daubigny's paintings were characterized by their emphasis on light, atmosphere, and mood, and his works often portrayed the beauty of the French countryside.

Jacob Lawrence was an American painter known for his genre paintings and figure paintings that depicted the African American experience and history. He was a prominent figure in the Harlem Renaissance, a cultural movement that celebrated African American art, literature, and music. Lawrence's artworks were characterized by their bold colors, dynamic compositions, and narrative storytelling, and they often portrayed the struggles and triumphs of the African American community.

Andre Derain was a French painter known for his landscape art and his association with the fauvism movement. He was known for his bold and vibrant use of color, which distinguished his works from traditional landscape paintings. Derain's artworks were characterized by their energetic brushwork, expressive use of color, and a sense of spontaneity and emotion.

Bert Hardy was a British photographer known for his photojournalistic and documentary works. He was renowned for his candid and humanistic approach to photography, capturing everyday life and the human condition with sensitivity and compassion. Hardy's photographs were characterized by their powerful storytelling, emotional depth, and social commentary.

Élisabeth Vigée Le Brun was a French painter known for her rococo style and portrait paintings. She was one of the few female painters of her time to gain recognition and success, and her portraits depicted members of the French aristocracy and high society. Vigée Le Brun's artworks were characterized by their delicate brushwork, graceful compositions, and attention to detail, and they often conveyed a sense of elegance and refinement.

Jeremy Geddes is a contemporary painter known for his unique and surreal artworks that often depict futuristic and otherworldly scenes. He is known for his highly detailed and meticulously rendered paintings that often feature solitary figures in urban environments, exploring themes of isolation, longing, and the passage of time. Geddes' artworks are characterized by their precise and realistic style, juxtaposed with fantastical elements, creating a sense of unease and mystery.

Peter Wileman is a British visual artist known for his bold and vibrant abstract artworks. He is known for his expressive and gestural brushwork, creating dynamic compositions that convey a sense of movement and energy. Wileman's artworks often feature landscapes, seascapes, and cityscapes, and are characterized by their bold use of color, bold shapes, and a sense of spontaneity and emotion.

Ary Scheffer was a French painter known for his history paintings and his role in the Romantic movement. He was known for his emotionally charged and dramatic depictions of historical events and biblical stories, often with a strong emphasis on human emotions and sentiments. Scheffer's paintings were characterized by their rich color palette, dynamic compositions, and a sense of theatricality and sentimentality.

Coles Phillips was an American artist known for his illustrations and advertisements. He was known for his distinctive "fadeaway" technique, in which he used negative space and subtle color transitions to create an illusion of figures blending into their backgrounds. Phillips' artworks were characterized by their innovative and creative use of composition and color, creating visually captivating and intriguing images.

Francis Bacon was a British painter known for his figurative art and surrealistic depictions of the human form. He was known for his bold and expressive use of color and texture, creating powerful and haunting images that often conveyed a sense of psychological and emotional intensity. Bacon's artworks were characterized by their distorted and twisted representations of the human body, often exploring themes of existentialism, mortality, and the human condition.

Olafur Eliasson is a Danish-Icelandic artist known for his abstract art and installation artworks. He is known for his immersive and experiential installations that often play with light, color, and perception. Eliasson's artworks are characterized by their interactive and participatory nature, inviting viewers to engage with the artworks and experience them in a sensory and contemplative way.

Eric Wallis is a researcher, but the specific field or area of research is not mentioned in the prompt.

Alexander Millar is a Scottish artist known for his paintings of working-class life, particularly his depictions of "gadgies," which are elderly working-class men from the northeast of England. He is known for his nostalgic and sentimental portrayal of these characters, capturing their humanity, resilience, and sense of community. Millar's artworks are characterized by their loose and expressive brushwork, warm color palette, and a sense of affection and empathy towards his subjects.

Andre Kertesz was a Hungarian-born photographer known for his influential and groundbreaking works in the field of photography. He is considered one of the pioneers of modern photography, known for his innovative use of composition, light, and shadow. Kertesz's photographs were characterized by their poetic and introspective nature, capturing the beauty of everyday life and the human condition in a deeply personal and emotive way.

Peter Mohrbacher is a contemporary visual artist known for his fantasy and surreal artworks. He is known for his imaginative and otherworldly depictions of fantastical creatures, ethereal landscapes, and dreamlike scenes. Mohrbacher's artworks are characterized by their intricate and detailed rendering, rich color palette, and a sense of magic and wonder.

Jean-Michel Basquiat was an American artist known for his figurative art and his contributions to the neo-expressionist movement. He was known for his bold and energetic paintings that often combined text, symbols, and vibrant colors, creating a raw and powerful visual language. Basquiat's artworks often explored social and political issues, including race, identity, and inequality, and were characterized by their frenetic brushwork, dynamic compositions, and a unique blend of graffiti, street art, and fine art aesthetics.

Akseli Gallen-Kallela was a Finnish painter known for his symbolism and romanticism-inspired artworks. He was known for his mystical and poetic depictions of nature, folklore, and national identity. Gallen-Kallela's artworks often featured rich symbolism, vivid color palette, and a sense of spirituality and mysticism, reflecting his deep connection to Finnish culture and mythology.

George Tooker was an American painter known for his meticulous and haunting depictions of contemporary life. He was known for his precise and detailed style, often depicting surreal and enigmatic scenes that explored the human condition and social issues. Tooker's artworks were characterized by their subtle use of color, precise rendering of forms, and a sense of psychological depth and emotional intensity.

Stevan Dohanos was an American painter known for his realistic depictions of everyday American life. His artworks often depicted scenes of rural America, small-town life, and American patriotism, capturing the spirit of mid-20th century America. Dohanos' paintings were characterized by their detailed and meticulous technique, vibrant colors, and nostalgic charm.

Diane Arbus was an American photographer known for her unique and controversial portraits. She is considered one of the pioneers of portrait photography and is known for her candid and often raw portrayals of people from marginalized communities, including individuals with physical and mental disabilities, transgender individuals, and people on the fringes of society. Arbus' photographs were characterized by their bold and provocative approach, challenging societal norms and conventions.

Sofonisba Anguissola was an Italian painter known for her genre paintings and portraits. She was one of the first prominent female artists of the Renaissance and is known for her delicate and intimate portrayals of people, capturing their personalities and emotions. Anguissola's artworks were characterized by their skillful technique, naturalistic style, and attention to detail.

James Abbott McNeill Whistler was an American-born painter known for his landscape art and marine art. He was a prominent figure in the Aesthetic movement and is known for his atmospheric and harmonious depictions of nature, often focusing on the play of light and color. Whistler's artworks were characterized by their subtle color palette, soft brushwork, and poetic sensibility.

Igor Morski is a contemporary Polish artist known for his surreal and thought-provoking artworks. He is known for his skillful digital manipulations and photorealistic style, creating imaginative and dreamlike compositions that often explore philosophical, psychological, and societal concepts. Morski's artworks are characterized by their intricate details, visual symbolism, and thought-provoking narratives.

Ray Caesar is a Canadian painter known for his digital art and surrealist style. He is known for his fantastical and otherworldly depictions of human figures, often blending elements of fantasy, mythology, and technology. Caesar's artworks are characterized by their meticulous details, imaginative compositions, and a sense of mystery and wonder.

Pierre Bonnard was a French painter known for his landscape art and association with the Nabis, a group of Post-Impressionist artists. He is known for his vibrant and colorful depictions of everyday life, capturing the fleeting moments of domestic scenes, gardens, and interiors. Bonnard's artworks were characterized by their bold use of color, loose brushwork, and intimate and personal approach to subject matter.

Helene Schjerfbeck was a Finnish painter known for her naturalistic and introspective style. She is considered one of the most important Finnish artists and is known for her sensitive and psychological portraits, self-portraits, and landscapes. Schjerfbeck's artworks were characterized by their muted color palette, subtle brushwork, and emotional depth.

Gerda Wegener was a Danish painter known for her portraits and association with the Art Deco movement. She is known for her sensual and glamorous depictions of women, often portraying them in fashionable clothing and luxurious settings. Wegener's artworks were characterized by their elegant style, attention to detail, and celebration of femininity.

Paolo Veronese was an Italian painter of the Venetian School known for his allegorical and mythological paintings. He is considered one of the most important painters of the Renaissance and is known for his grand and dramatic compositions, rich color palette, and skillful rendering of human figures. Veronese's artworks were characterized by their theatricality, opulence, and narrative storytelling.

Pieter Bruegel the Elder was a Flemish painter known for his landscape art and genre paintings. He is considered one of the most important painters of the Northern Renaissance and is known for his detailed and panoramic depictions of rural life, folklore, and human behavior. Bruegel's artworks were characterized by their meticulous attention to detail, rich symbolism, and masterful composition.

Anne-Louis Girodet was a French painter known for his mythological paintings and association with the Romanticism movement. He is known for his sensual and emotive portrayals of mythological and historical subjects, often capturing intense emotions and dramatic narratives. Girodet's artworks were characterized by their vivid color palette, dynamic compositions, and poetic sensibility.

John Duncan was a Scottish painter known for his intricate and detailed artworks, often depicting mythological and allegorical subjects. In addition to being a painter, Duncan was also a neurologist, and his scientific knowledge often influenced his artworks. His paintings were characterized by their meticulous details, luminous colors, and fantastical imagery.

Paul Corfield is a contemporary British artist known for his mixed-media artworks, often featuring urban landscapes and cityscapes. He is known for his unique and experimental approach to art, incorporating various techniques and materials to create multi-layered and textured compositions. Corfield's artworks are characterized by their abstract and expressive style, capturing the energy and vibrancy of urban environments.

Gaston Bussière was a French painter known for his symbolist artworks. He is considered one of the key figures of the symbolist movement in France and is known for his mystical and allegorical depictions of fantastical subjects, often exploring spiritual and philosophical themes. Bussière's artworks were characterized by their dreamlike quality, mysterious symbolism, and poetic atmosphere.

Flora Borsi is a contemporary Hungarian artist known for her unique and imaginative artworks. She is known for her digital manipulations and conceptual approach to art, often blending elements of photography, painting, and digital art to create visually stunning and thought-provoking compositions. Borsi's artworks are characterized by their surreal and fantastical elements, inviting viewers to question reality and perception.

Howard Pyle was an American writer and illustrator known for his association with the Brandywine School, a group of artists known for their illustrations of American history and literature. Pyle is considered one of the most influential illustrators of the late 19th and early 20th centuries and is known for his dynamic and narrative-driven artworks, capturing scenes of adventure, heroism, and historical events. His illustrations were characterized by their dramatic composition, rich details, and emotional impact.

Eduardo Kobra is a Brazilian street artist known for his large-scale murals and colorful artworks. He is known for his vibrant and bold style, often incorporating cultural and historical references in his murals. Kobra's artworks are characterized by their intricate details, vivid colors, and celebration of diversity and social issues.

Edwin Henry Landseer was a British painter known for his romantic and sentimental artworks, often featuring animals as central subjects. He is known for his skillful rendering of animals and capturing their personalities and emotions, often anthropomorphizing them in his paintings. Landseer's artworks were characterized by their realistic and detailed style, capturing the beauty and charm of animals in a sentimental and sometimes humorous manner.

Odd Nerdrum is a Norwegian painter known for his figurative art and association with the Kitsch movement. He is known for his deeply emotional and often provocative portrayals of human figures, often exploring existential and philosophical themes. Nerdrum's artworks were characterized by their detailed and precise technique, moody and mysterious atmospheres, and thought-provoking narratives.

Alberto Giacometti was a Swiss sculptor known for his abstract art and association with the Surrealist and Existentialist movements. He is known for his elongated and emaciated human figures, often depicting the human form in a raw and existential manner, reflecting the anxieties and uncertainties of the human condition. Giacometti's sculptures were characterized by their distinctively thin and elongated forms, rough and textured surfaces, and a sense of isolation and alienation.

Edmund Dulac was a French-born British painter known for his Orientalist artworks, often depicting scenes from the Middle East and Asia. He is known for his exotic and fantastical portrayals of Oriental subjects, capturing the richness and mystique of these cultures. Dulac's artworks were characterized by their vibrant colors, intricate details, and a sense of exoticism and escapism.

Takashi Murakami is a contemporary Japanese artist known for his figurative art and sculptural works. He is known for his fusion of traditional Japanese art techniques with contemporary pop culture, creating whimsical and colorful artworks that blur the boundaries between high and low art. Murakami's artworks are characterized by their vibrant colors, playful imagery, and a sense of youthful energy and optimism.

John Currin is an American painter known for his contemporary art and provocative portrayals of the human figure. He is known for his skillful and detailed renderings of human anatomy, often in exaggerated and distorted forms, exploring themes of sexuality, gender, and social norms. Currin's artworks are characterized by their provocative and sometimes controversial subject matter, meticulous technique, and a combination of classical and modern influences.

Robert McCall was an American artist known for his illustrations of space exploration and science fiction subjects. He is known for his realistic and imaginative depictions of space travel, planetary landscapes, and futuristic concepts, capturing the wonder and awe of the unknown universe. McCall's artworks were characterized by their detailed and precise style, depicting a vision of space that inspired generations of space enthusiasts.

Artemisia Gentileschi was an Italian Baroque painter known for her mythological paintings and portraits. She is known for her strong and powerful depictions of female figures, often exploring themes of female empowerment, resilience, and justice. Gentileschi's artworks were characterized by their dramatic composition, intense emotions, and a distinctive use of chiaroscuro, creating a sense of depth and drama in her paintings.

Guo Pei is a Chinese fashion designer known for her extravagant and intricate couture creations. She is known for her bold use of colors, luxurious fabrics, and intricate craftsmanship, creating breathtaking and unique designs that blend traditional Chinese aesthetics with modern fashion sensibilities. Guo Pei's designs have been worn by celebrities and showcased in prestigious fashion events, garnering international recognition for her innovative and artistic approach to fashion.

Bartolome Esteban Murillo was a Spanish Baroque painter known for his genre paintings, depicting everyday life scenes with a naturalistic and empathetic approach. He is known for his ability to capture the emotions and expressions of his subjects, creating intimate and poignant portrayals of people from different social classes. Murillo's artworks were characterized by their rich color palette, soft brushwork, and a sense of humanity and compassion.

Raja Ravi Varma was an Indian painter known for his portraits and depictions of Indian mythology and epic stories. He is known for his realistic and detailed portrayals of figures from Indian folklore and history, capturing their emotions and stories with great finesse. Raja Ravi Varma's artworks were characterized by their vibrant colors, intricate details, and a sense of grandeur and beauty.

Adrian Smith is an English heavy metal guitarist known for his work with the band Iron Maiden. He is known for his powerful and melodic guitar playing, contributing to the iconic sound of Iron Maiden and influencing generations of heavy metal guitarists. Smith's playing style is characterized by his intricate solos, catchy riffs, and a sense of emotion and passion in his performances.

Honoré Daumier was a French artist known for his caricatures and social commentary through his art. He is known for his satirical depictions of the French society and political scene of his time, using wit and humor to highlight the flaws and absurdities of human nature. Daumier's artworks were characterized by their sharp wit, expressive lines, and a keen observation of human behavior.

Remedios Varo was a Spanish Mexican surrealist painter known for her imaginative and dreamlike artworks. She is known for her detailed and mysterious depictions of fantastical worlds and surreal scenarios, often featuring enigmatic female figures. Varo's artworks were characterized by their intricate details, symbolic imagery, and a sense of mysticism and enchantment.

Ernst Haeckel was a German biologist and artist known for his detailed illustrations of marine life and natural history subjects. He is known for his scientific illustrations, capturing the intricacies and beauty of the natural world with great precision. Haeckel's artworks were characterized by their meticulous attention to detail, scientific accuracy, and a sense of wonder and fascination for the diversity of life.

Bess Hamiti is an Albanian artist known for her contemporary art and experimental approach to various mediums. She is known for her unique and thought-provoking artworks that challenge traditional artistic boundaries and explore themes of identity, feminism, and cultural heritage. Hamiti's artworks are characterized by their experimental techniques, bold use of colors, and a thought-provoking narrative.

Marie Spartali Stillman was a British artist known for her landscape art and association with the Pre-Raphaelite Brotherhood. She is known for her romantic and lyrical depictions of natural landscapes, often inspired by her travels in Italy and Greece. Spartali Stillman's artworks were characterized by their ethereal and poetic quality, delicate brushwork, and a sense of emotional depth.

Albert Marquet was a French painter known for his Fauvist artworks, characterized by their bold use of color and simplified forms. He is known for his vibrant and expressive landscapes, cityscapes, and seascapes, capturing the essence of the scenes with dynamic and vivid brushwork. Marquet's artworks were characterized by their bold and daring color palette, loose and gestural brushstrokes, and a sense of spontaneity and energy.

Jeanloup Sieff was a French photographer known for his fashion, portrait, and nude photography. He is known for his distinctive and sensual style, capturing the human form with elegance and grace. Sieff's photographs were characterized by their strong composition, play of light and shadow, and a sense of intimacy and sensuality.

Ismail Inceoglu is a Turkish artist known for his contemporary art and exploration of cultural identity. He is known for his mixed-media artworks that combine traditional Turkish motifs with modern artistic techniques, creating unique and thought-provoking pieces. Inceoglu's artworks were characterized by their intricate details, rich symbolism, and a fusion of traditional and contemporary elements.

Berndnaut Smilde is a Dutch sculptor known for his innovative approach to sculpture and installation art. He is known for his "Nimbus" series, where he creates clouds indoors using smoke and humidity, capturing a fleeting and ethereal moment in a solid form. Smilde's artworks were characterized by their ephemeral and transient nature, blurring the boundaries between art, science, and nature.

Donato Giancola is an American artist known for his science fiction and fantasy-themed paintings. He is known for his highly detailed and realistic artworks, depicting epic battles, heroic figures, and imaginative worlds. Giancola's paintings were characterized by their masterful technique, attention to detail, and a sense of epic storytelling.

Guillermo del Toro is a Mexican filmmaker known for his psychological thrillers and horror films. He is known for his visually stunning and emotionally resonant films, often exploring themes of fantasy, horror, and the supernatural. Del Toro's films were characterized by their intricate and imaginative storytelling, rich visual aesthetics, and a deep emotional connection with the audience.

Bill Brandt was a British photographer known for his symbolic and surrealist-inspired photographs. He is known for his unique and poetic approach to photography, capturing the surreal and otherworldly aspects of everyday life. Brandt's photographs were characterized by their dramatic contrasts, unconventional compositions, and a sense of mystery and intrigue.

Santiago Calatrava is a Spanish architect known for his high-tech architecture and sculptural designs. He is known for his innovative and futuristic buildings, characterized by their sleek and elegant forms, extensive use of glass and steel, and a sense of movement and fluidity. Calatrava's sculptures are also renowned for their dynamic and organic shapes, often resembling natural elements like birds, wings, and waves.

Marco Mazzoni is an Italian artist known for his intricate and detailed colored pencil drawings. He is known for his botanical illustrations and depictions of animals, often drawing inspiration from folklore, mythology, and the natural world. Mazzoni's artworks are characterized by their meticulous attention to detail, vibrant color palette, and a sense of mystery and symbolism.

Cyril Rolando, also known as "AquaSixio," is a French digital artist known for his imaginative and surreal artworks. He is known for his dreamlike and fantastical illustrations, often depicting whimsical characters and scenes with a touch of melancholy. Rolando's artworks are characterized by their surreal and otherworldly quality, rich symbolism, and a unique blend of digital and traditional artistic techniques.

Craig Davison is a British artist known for his nostalgic and whimsical paintings. He is known for his depictions of childhood memories and pop culture references, often capturing moments of imagination and adventure. Davison's artworks are characterized by their nostalgic and evocative quality, with a touch of humor and playfulness.

Richard Burlet is a French artist known for his expressive and abstract paintings. He is known for his bold and vibrant use of color, dynamic brushwork, and unique artistic style that combines elements of abstraction and figuration. Burlet's artworks are characterized by their energetic and emotional quality, inviting viewers to interpret and experience the emotions and sensations portrayed in his paintings.

Victor Nizovtsev is a Russian painter known for his enchanting and fantastical artworks. He is known for his depictions of whimsical and magical scenes, often featuring fairy tale-like characters and landscapes. Nizovtsev's paintings are characterized by their luminous and ethereal quality, rich details, and a sense of wonder and imagination.

Roger Dean is a British illustrator known for his iconic album cover designs and fantasy artworks. He is known for his imaginative and otherworldly landscapes, often featuring fantastical creatures, intricate details, and a sense of mystical and dreamlike atmosphere. Dean's artworks are characterized by their fantastical and surreal quality, making him one of the most influential illustrators in the field of music and fantasy art.

Norman Foster is a British architect known for his pioneering work in high-tech architecture and sustainable design. He is known for his innovative and iconic buildings, characterized by their cutting-edge technologies, sleek and minimalistic forms, and a strong emphasis on sustainability and environmental consciousness. Foster's architectural designs have redefined modern architecture and have had a significant impact on the urban landscape around the world.

Joseph Lorusso is an American painter known for his figurative and emotionally charged artworks. He is known for his depictions of intimate and introspective moments, often capturing the human condition and emotions with sensitivity and depth. Lorusso's paintings are characterized by their emotional and psychological intensity, with a focus on the human figure and its expressions.

Aron Wiesenfeld is an American artist known for his evocative and atmospheric paintings, often drawing inspiration from mythology, fairy tales, and the natural world. He is known for his highly detailed and narrative-driven artworks, capturing moments of solitude and reflection. Wiesenfeld's paintings are characterized by their introspective and emotive quality, inviting viewers to contemplate the stories and emotions depicted in his works.

Zinaida Serebriakova was a Russian painter known for her portraits, genre scenes, and self-portraits. She is considered one of the most significant female artists in Russian art history.

Serebriakova's artworks are characterized by their exquisite technique, attention to detail, and a sense of intimacy and warmth. Her portraits often capture the inner world of her subjects, reflecting their personalities, emotions, and surroundings.

Marc Simonetti is a French illustrator known for his stunning and immersive fantasy artworks. He is known for his illustrations of fantastical worlds, creatures, and characters, often inspired by literature and mythology. Simonetti's artworks are characterized by their intricate details, rich colors, and a sense of grandeur and epic storytelling.

James Paick is a Korean-American concept artist and illustrator known for his concept designs for video games and films. He is known for his imaginative and futuristic artworks, often depicting futuristic cities, vehicles, and environments. Paick's artworks are characterized by their dynamic and cinematic quality, with a keen attention to perspective, lighting, and composition.

Sam Spratt is an American artist known for his digital paintings and illustrations. He is known for his hyper-realistic and detailed artworks, often featuring portraits of celebrities and pop culture figures. Spratt's artworks are characterized by their meticulous attention to detail, striking use of color and lighting, and a sense of depth and realism.

Andreas Rocha is a Portuguese artist known for his stunning landscape paintings. He is known for his atmospheric and emotive artworks, often depicting serene natural scenes and fantastical landscapes. Rocha's paintings are characterized by their breathtaking beauty, rich color palette, and a sense of tranquility and wonder.

James Jean is a Taiwanese-American painter known for his surreal and ethereal artworks. He is known for his dreamlike and otherworldly paintings, often featuring fantastical creatures, dreamscapes, and surreal elements. Jean's artworks are characterized by their delicate and intricate details, imaginative compositions, and a sense of mysticism and mystery.

Michael Whelan is an American artist known for his illustrations and paintings in the genres of science fiction and fantasy art. He is known for his detailed and imaginative artworks, often depicting otherworldly landscapes, creatures, and characters. Whelan's artworks are characterized by their fantastical and immersive quality, with a strong emphasis on lighting, composition, and storytelling.

M.C. Escher was a Dutch artist known for his unique and mind-bending artworks that combine elements of abstract art, cityscapes, and mathematical concepts. He is known for his intricate and illusionary drawings, often depicting impossible geometries, tessellations, and metamorphoses. Escher's artworks are characterized by their precise and meticulous technique, optical illusions, and a sense of intellectual curiosity and exploration.

Frank Frazetta was an American painter known for his iconic and powerful artworks in the genre of fantasy art. He is known for his dynamic and muscular depictions of heroic characters, fierce creatures, and epic battle scenes. Frazetta's artworks are characterized by their bold and vibrant use of color, dramatic lighting, and a sense of action and adventure.

Serge Marshennikov is a Russian painter known for his stunningly realistic and intimate portraits of women. He is known for his masterful technique and attention to detail, capturing the delicate beauty and sensuality of his female subjects. Marshennikov's paintings are characterized by their exquisite and luminous quality, with a focus on the human figure and its emotions.

Louis Icart was a French painter known for his elegant and sensual depictions of the female form. He is known for his glamorous and stylish artworks, often depicting women in luxurious settings, adorned with fashionable clothing and accessories. Icart's paintings are characterized by their romantic and nostalgic quality, capturing the spirit of the Art Deco era and the allure of the modern woman.

Albert O Vargas was a Peruvian-American painter known for his pin-up and glamour art. He is known for his sensual and alluring depictions of women, often featuring them in provocative poses and glamorous attire. Vargas' paintings are characterized by their exquisite attention to detail, lush use of color, and a sense of elegance and sophistication.

Frank Gehry is a Canadian American architect known for his groundbreaking and innovative designs in the field of architecture, particularly in the realm of postmodern architecture. He is known for his bold and unconventional use of materials, unique forms, and complex geometries. Gehry's architectural designs are characterized by their iconic and sculptural quality, pushing the boundaries of traditional architectural conventions, and creating iconic landmarks.

Frederick McCubbin was an Australian painter known for his landscape art and depictions of Australian bush life. He is known for his atmospheric and evocative artworks, often depicting serene natural scenes and the daily life of early Australian settlers. McCubbin's paintings are characterized by their realistic and detailed portrayal of the Australian landscape, capturing the unique light, colors, and mood of the Australian bush.

John Howe is an English illustrator known for his contributions to fantasy literature, particularly for his illustrations of J.R.R. Tolkien's Middle earth. He is known for his intricate and detailed artworks, often depicting scenes from Tolkien's novels and other fantasy works. Howe's illustrations are characterized by their rich and imaginative depictions of fantasy worlds, creatures, and landscapes, capturing the spirit of Tolkien's storytelling.

Shaun Tan is an Australian writer and illustrator known for his unique and thought-provoking artworks in the field of children's literature and graphic novels. He is known for his distinctive and surreal illustrations, often depicting fantastical worlds, allegorical stories, and emotionally resonant themes. Tan's artworks are characterized by their deep emotional impact, intricate details, and thought-provoking storytelling.

Dora Maar was a French photographer known for her avant-garde and surrealist works. She is known for her experimental and provocative photographs, often exploring the boundaries of traditional photography and pushing the limits of artistic expression. Maar's photographs are characterized by their dreamlike and surreal quality, often featuring unconventional subjects, perspectives, and techniques.

Giorgio De Chirico was an Italian artist known for his pioneering role in the development of abstract art and his unique depictions of cityscapes. He is known for his enigmatic and metaphysical artworks, often featuring deserted urban landscapes, mysterious shadows, and enigmatic objects. De Chirico's paintings are characterized by their dreamlike and introspective quality, challenging the traditional notions of space, time, and reality.

Georges de La Tour was a French painter known for his classicism and genre painting. He is known for his detailed and realistic depictions of everyday life, often featuring ordinary people in domestic scenes, taverns, and candlelit interiors. De La Tour's paintings are characterized by their subtle use of light and shadow, exquisite attention to detail, and a sense of intimacy and warmth.

Anthony Thieme was a Dutch American painter known for his vibrant and impressionistic artworks. He is known for his plein air paintings, often depicting coastal scenes, landscapes, and seascapes. Thieme's paintings are characterized by their bold and expressive brushwork, brilliant use of color, and a sense of spontaneity and energy.

Alex Andreev is a Russian painter known for his surreal and atmospheric artworks. He is known for his imaginative and otherworldly paintings, often featuring surreal landscapes, dreamscapes, and strange creatures. Andreev's artworks are characterized by their haunting and mysterious quality, with a sense of depth and atmosphere that draws the viewer into a surreal and fantastical world.

Thomas Saliot is a French painter known for his evocative and emotive artworks. He is known for his figurative and narrative paintings, often depicting intimate moments, human emotions, and the beauty of the natural world. Saliot's paintings are characterized by their rich use of color, expressive brushwork, and a sense of poetic storytelling.

Louis Janmot was a French painter known for his romantic and spiritual artworks. He is known for his allegorical and symbolic paintings, often depicting religious and mythological themes. Janmot's paintings are characterized by their poetic and emotional quality, with a sense of spirituality and mysticism that transcends the physical realm.

Laurie Lipton is an American artist known for her intricate and detailed artworks. She is known for her black and white drawings, often featuring macabre and fantastical themes. Lipton's artworks are characterized by their meticulous attention to detail, dark and surreal imagery, and a sense of mystery and intrigue.

Casey Weldon is as an American artist. He is known for his surreal and often humorous artworks that blend elements of pop culture, nostalgia, and the macabre. Weldon's artworks often feature strange and whimsical characters, often with a dark twist, and are characterized by their vibrant colors, intricate details, and unique visual storytelling.

Hyacinthe Rigaud was a French painter known for his portraits during the Baroque period. He is known for his lavish and detailed portraits of royalty, aristocrats, and prominent figures of his time. Rigaud's portraits are characterized by their grandeur, meticulous attention to detail, and use of dramatic lighting to create a sense of nobility and prestige.

Alson Skinner Clark was an American painter known for his landscape artworks. He is known for his realistic and detailed paintings of the American West, particularly the desert landscapes of Arizona and New Mexico. Clark's landscape paintings are characterized by their sweeping vistas, vivid colors, and a sense of awe and reverence for the natural world.

Mikhail Nesterov was a Russian painter known for his landscape and religious artworks. He is known for his romantic and mystical paintings, often depicting scenes from Russian history, folklore, and mythology. Nesterov's artworks are characterized by their spiritual and emotional depth, with a sense of otherworldliness and poetic symbolism.

Konstantin Korovin was a Russian painter known for his versatile talents and wide range of subjects, including landscape, still life, and genre painting. He is known for his impressionistic style, often depicting scenes from everyday life, landscapes, and still life compositions with vibrant colors and bold brushwork.

Otto Dix was a German painter known for his provocative and often controversial artworks. He is known for his scathing social critique and satirical depictions of war, politics, and society. Dix's artworks often feature dark and disturbing imagery, including mythological themes, with a critical eye towards the human condition and the horrors of war.

Iain Faulkner is a Scottish painter known for his realistic and atmospheric artworks. He is known for his figurative paintings, often depicting solitary figures in moody and introspective settings. Faulkner's artworks are characterized by their meticulous attention to detail, subtle use of light and shadow, and a sense of solitude and contemplation.

Alfred Munnings was an English painter known for his equestrian and sporting artworks. He is known for his dynamic and lively paintings of horses, riders, and racing scenes. Munnings' artworks are characterized by their energetic brushwork, sense of movement, and a deep appreciation for the beauty and grace of horses.

Karol Bak is a Polish painter known for his realistic and detailed artworks, often depicting scenes from nature and landscapes. Bak's paintings are characterized by their meticulous attention to detail, rich colors, and atmospheric lighting.

Antony Gormley is a British artist known for his figurative artworks and contemporary art. He is best known for his sculptures and installations that explore the human body and its relationship to space and the environment. Gormley's artworks often challenge traditional notions of sculpture and provoke introspection and reflection on the human condition.

Rebeca Saray is a Spanish photographer and artist known for her unique style that blends fantasy, surrealism, and conceptual elements. Her artworks often feature dreamlike and fantastical compositions, with a focus on storytelling and emotive expressions.

Antoni Gaudi was a renowned Catalan architect known for his distinctive style of Catalan Modernism. He is best known for his iconic buildings in Barcelona, including the Sagrada Familia, Casa Batlló, and Park Güell. Gaudi's architecture is characterized by its intricate organic forms, use of colorful ceramics, and a harmonious integration of natural elements.

Henry Asencio is an American painter known for his emotive and expressive portrait paintings. He is known for his unique style that combines elements of realism and abstraction, creating dynamic and emotionally charged artworks.

Carrie Mae Weems is an American artist known for her social-artistic projects and installation art. She uses various mediums, including photography, video, and text, to explore issues of race, gender, and identity. Weems' artworks are often thought-provoking, challenging societal norms and addressing important social and cultural issues.

Brent Cotton is an American painter known for his atmospheric and evocative landscape artworks. He is known for his impressionistic style, capturing the beauty and serenity of the natural world through his paintings. Cotton's artworks are characterized by their lush colors, expressive brushwork, and a sense of tranquility.

Kim Keever is an American artist known for his unique approach to landscape art. He creates his landscapes by constructing miniature dioramas in his studio, which he then floods with water and adds various pigments to create stunning and ephemeral underwater landscapes. Keever's artworks are characterized by their dreamlike quality, with a sense of mystery and wonder.

Thomas Allom was a British architect known for his work in the 19th century, particularly in the field of architectural illustration. He is known for his detailed engravings and drawings of historic buildings, landscapes, and cityscapes, capturing the beauty and grandeur of architectural landmarks.

Gabriele Münter was a German painter associated with the expressionist movement, known for her cityscape and portrait paintings. She was a member of the Blue Rider movement, which advocated for the use of bold colors and expressive forms in art. Münter's artworks are characterized by their vibrant colors, dynamic brushwork, and emotional intensity.

Johann Wolfgang von Goethe was a German writer, poet, and theater manager known for his contributions to German literature and the Sturm und Drang movement. He is considered one of the most important literary figures in Western history, known for his influential works such as "Faust" and his significant impact on German culture and literature.

Piet Mondrian was a Dutch painter known for his abstract art and pioneering role in the development of the De Stijl art movement. He is known for his iconic compositions of rectangles and primary colors, which represent his vision of universal harmony and abstraction of reality.

John James Audubon was an American ornithologist, naturalist, and painter known for his landscape and animal paintings. He is best known for his monumental work "The Birds of America," a collection of detailed and lifelike illustrations of North American birds Jessica Rossier is an artist known for her unique and imaginative artworks that blend elements of fantasy, mythology, and surrealism. She often creates whimsical and otherworldly compositions, with a focus on intricate details and a dreamlike quality.

Adolph Menzel was a German painter known for his contributions to realism in art. He is known for his meticulous and detailed paintings that capture everyday life and historical events with a keen eye for accuracy and detail. Menzel's artworks often depict scenes from 19th-century German society and are characterized by their technical skill and attention to atmospheric lighting.

Thomas Blackshear is an American painter known for his striking and emotive artworks, often depicting African-American culture and history. He is known for his skillful use of color, light, and shadow to create powerful and thought-provoking compositions that convey deep emotions and narratives.

Paul Klee was a Swiss-German artist known for his abstract art and surrealism. He was a prominent figure in the Bauhaus art movement and is known for his innovative use of color, line, and geometric forms in his artworks. Klee's artworks often have a whimsical and playful quality, with a sense of childlike wonder and experimentation.

Kazimir Malevich was a Russian avant-garde artist known for his contributions to abstract art and figurative art. He is best known for his iconic painting "Black Square," which is considered a seminal work of abstract art. Malevich's artworks are characterized by their bold use of color and geometric forms, challenging traditional notions of representation and pushing the boundaries of artistic expression.

Ian McQue is a British artist known for his imaginative and detailed artworks that often depict futuristic and dystopian scenes. He is known for his unique style that combines elements of steampunk, industrial design, and science fiction, creating captivating and immersive worlds through his artworks.

Bruce Pennington is a British painter known for his evocative and otherworldly artworks. He is known for his distinct style that combines elements of surrealism, fantasy, and science fiction, often depicting futuristic landscapes and imaginative worlds. Pennington's artworks are characterized by their rich colors, intricate details, and a sense of mystery and wonder.

Michael Carson is an American artist known for his unique and expressive paintings that often explore the human figure and emotions. He is known for his skillful use of brushwork and color, creating dynamic and emotionally charged compositions that capture the human form with a sense of intimacy and sensitivity.

Eugene von Guerard was an Austrian-born Australian painter known for his landscape artworks. He is known for his detailed and precise paintings of the Australian landscape, capturing the beauty and diversity of the Australian wilderness with a keen eye for naturalistic details. Von Guerard's artworks are characterized by their meticulous attention to detail, atmospheric lighting, and a sense of awe and reverence for nature.

Michelangelo Merisi Da Caravaggio was an Italian painter known for his genre paintings and contributions to the Baroque art movement. He is known for his innovative use of light and shadow, known as chiaroscuro, and his realistic depictions of everyday life and ordinary people. Caravaggio's artworks are characterized by their dramatic and emotive compositions, with a focus on naturalistic details and a bold use of light and shadow.

Jean Fouquet was a French painter known for his contributions to the Renaissance art movement. He is known for his detailed and precise portrait paintings, capturing the likeness and personality of his subjects with a keen eye for detail and expression. Fouquet's artworks are characterized by their meticulous brushwork, rich colors, and a sense of depth and dimensionality.

Sou Fujimoto is a Japanese architect known for his innovative and experimental approach to architecture. He is known for his unique and conceptual designs that challenge traditional notions of space, structure, and function in architecture. Fujimoto's architectural designs often blur the lines between interior and exterior, creating dynamic and interactive spaces that push the boundaries of traditional architectural forms.

Naoto Hattori is an American artist known for his surreal and imaginative artworks. He is known for his unique style that combines elements of fantasy, science fiction, and the natural world, creating whimsical and dreamlike compositions. Hattori's artworks are characterized by their intricate details, vibrant colors, and a sense of mystery and wonder.

Carl Gustav Carus was a German landscape artist and botanist known for his contributions to landscape art. He is known for his detailed and realistic landscape paintings, capturing the beauty and serenity of nature with a keen scientific eye. Carus's artworks often depict botanical specimens with meticulous accuracy, showcasing his deep knowledge and passion for botany.

Simeon Solomon was an English artist known for his contributions to the Pre-Raphaelite Brotherhood and his history paintings. He is known for his richly detailed and emotionally charged artworks that often depict biblical and mythological themes, exploring themes of spirituality, desire, and forbidden love. Solomon's artworks are characterized by their exquisite attention to detail, vibrant colors, and a sense of poetic melancholy.

Tyler Shields is an American photographer known for his provocative and edgy photographic works. He is known for his bold and controversial images that challenge societal norms and push the boundaries of artistic expression. Shields's photographs often explore themes of identity, sexuality, and social commentary, capturing raw and powerful moments with a fearless and unapologetic approach.

Max Ernst was a German artist known for his contributions to abstract art and Dadaism. He is known for his innovative and experimental approach to art, creating surreal and dreamlike compositions that challenge traditional artistic techniques and conventions. Ernst's artworks often feature juxtapositions of different elements and unexpected combinations, creating a sense of disorientation and wonder.

Annibale Carracci was an Italian painter known for his genre paintings and contributions to the Baroque art movement. He is known for his skillful use of color and composition, creating dynamic and emotive artworks that capture everyday life and human emotions with sensitivity and realism. Carracci's artworks are characterized by their naturalistic details, vibrant colors, and a sense of theatricality.

Kelly Vivanco is an American painter known for her whimsical and narrative artworks. She is known for her unique style that combines elements of fantasy, storytelling, and surrealism, creating captivating and enchanting compositions. Vivanco's artworks often feature whimsical characters, animals, and nature, with a focus on storytelling and emotions.

Frederic Church was an American landscape artist known for his contributions to the Hudson River School of painting. He is known for his breathtaking and majestic landscape paintings that capture the sublime beauty of the American wilderness with a sense of awe and reverence. Church's artworks are characterized by their luminous colors, meticulous details, and a sense of grandeur and spirituality.

Nick Knight is a British photographer known for his innovative and avant-garde photographic works. He is known for his experimental approach to photography, pushing the boundaries of traditional photographic techniques and creating visually stunning and thought-provoking images. Knight's photographs often challenge societal norms and conventions, exploring themes of identity, beauty, and fashion with a bold and artistic vision.

Peter Gric is an Austrian painter known for his surreal and fantastical artworks. He is known for his intricate and detailed paintings that often depict surreal and dreamlike landscapes, blurring the lines between reality and fantasy. Gric's artworks are characterized by their rich colors, meticulous details, and a sense of mystery and wonder.

Tristan Eaton is an American muralist known for his large-scale and visually captivating murals. He is known for his bold and dynamic artworks that transform urban spaces with vibrant colors, intricate details, and engaging narratives. Eaton's murals often incorporate elements of pop culture, mythology, and social commentary, creating visually stunning and thought-provoking artworks that resonate with viewers.

Alex Timmermans is an American artist known for his contemporary abstract paintings. He is known for his bold and expressive use of color, texture, and form, creating dynamic and visually captivating compositions. Timmermans' artworks often evoke a sense of movement and energy, with a focus on abstract expressionism and gestural mark-making.

Kate Greenaway was an English painter known for her contributions to children's book illustrations. She is known for her charming and nostalgic artworks that depict scenes of childhood innocence, capturing the beauty of nature and everyday life with a delicate and whimsical touch. Greenaway's illustrations are characterized by their intricate details, soft colors, and a sense of warmth and nostalgia.

Arthur Lismer was a Canadian painter known for his contributions to the Group of Seven, a famous Canadian art movement. He is known for his landscape paintings that capture the rugged beauty of the Canadian wilderness with a bold and expressive style. Lismer's artworks often feature vibrant colors, dynamic compositions, and a sense of reverence for the Canadian landscape.

Théodore Géricault was a French painter known for his contributions to the Romanticism art movement. He is known for his emotionally charged and powerful artworks that depict scenes of drama, heroism, and human emotions. Géricault's artworks often feature dynamic compositions, intense colors, and a sense of theatricality, exploring themes of human psychology and the complexities of the human condition.

Pieter de Hooch was a Dutch painter known for his contributions to landscape art and genre painting. He is known for his meticulously detailed and beautifully composed artworks that capture scenes of everyday life with a sense of intimacy and warmth. De Hooch's paintings often feature tranquil domestic interiors, play of light and shadow, and human interactions, creating a sense of serenity and harmony.

John Salminen is an American painter known for his landscape artworks. He is known for his bold and expressive style that captures the beauty of urban landscapes with a unique perspective. Salminen's artworks often feature dramatic compositions, dynamic brushwork, and a sense of atmosphere, creating evocative and powerful representations of urban environments.

Stephan Martiniere is a French-American artist known for his contributions to concept art and science fiction illustration. He is known for his imaginative and futuristic artworks that depict otherworldly landscapes, cityscapes, and characters with a sense of wonder and awe. Martiniere's artworks often feature vibrant colors, intricate details, and a sense of storytelling, bringing to life fantastical worlds and visions of the future.

Max Dupain was an Australian photographer known for his contributions to modernist photography. He is known for his black-and-white photographs that capture the beauty of the Australian landscape, architecture, and people with a keen eye for composition and light. Dupain's photographs are characterized by their strong visual impact, use of contrast, and modernist aesthetic.

Coby Whitmore was an American illustrator known for his work in advertising, magazines, and book covers. He is known for his elegant and sophisticated illustrations that often depict scenes of everyday life, fashion, and romance. Whitmore's illustrations are characterized by their attention to detail, subtle use of color, and a sense of grace and refinement.

Edwin Austin Abbey was an American painter known for his contributions to the art of painting. He is known for his historical and literary-themed paintings that often depict scenes from Shakespearean plays, medieval literature, and the American Revolution. Abbey's paintings are characterized by their meticulous details, rich colors, and a sense of storytelling.

Filippino Lippi was an Italian Renaissance painter known for his contributions to the art world. He is known for his religious-themed paintings that often depict scenes from the Bible, classical mythology, and Italian history. Lippi's paintings are characterized by their exquisite technique, emotional depth, and masterful use of color and light.

Anish Kapoor is a British-Indian sculptor known for his abstract art and contemporary art. He is known for his large-scale sculptures that often explore the concepts of space, form, and perception. Kapoor's sculptures are characterized by their monumental size, sleek surfaces, and intriguing forms that challenge the viewer's perception of space and materiality.

Max Weber was an American artist known for his contributions to modern art and abstract expressionism. He is known for his bold and expressive paintings that often feature abstract and semi-abstract forms, vibrant colors, and dynamic compositions. Weber's artworks are characterized by their energetic brushwork, emotional intensity, and innovative approach to abstraction.

Ben Aronson is an American painter known for his abstract expressionist paintings. He is known for his dynamic and energetic artworks that often depict urban landscapes, cityscapes, and people in motion. Aronson's paintings are characterized by their bold brushwork, vibrant colors, and gestural marks that convey a sense of movement and vitality.

Irma Stern was a South African painter known for her contributions to modern art and genre painting. She is known for her vibrant and expressive artworks that often depict scenes from everyday life, portraits, and landscapes with a distinctive African flair. Stern's paintings are characterized by their bold use of color, loose brushwork, and a sense of emotional intensity.

John Berkey was an American painter known for his work in science fiction and fantasy art. He is known for his detailed and imaginative paintings that often depict futuristic cities, spaceships, and otherworldly landscapes. Berkey's artworks are characterized by their meticulous details, sense of scale, and a sense of wonder and adventure.

Beeple, whose real name is Mike Winkelmann, is a digital artist known for his contributions to visual art. He is known for his innovative and boundary-pushing artworks that often combine digital technology, social commentary, and pop culture references. Beeple's artworks are characterized by their surreal and thought-provoking imagery, intricate details, and futuristic aesthetics.

JC Leyendecker was an American illustrator known for his work in advertising, magazines, and book covers. He is known for his iconic and stylish illustrations that often depict scenes of fashion, sports, and everyday life with a distinctive Art Deco flair. Leyendecker's illustrations are characterized by their bold use of color, attention to detail, and a sense of elegance and sophistication.

Vhils, whose real name is Alexandre Farto, is a Portuguese street artist known for his contributions to muralism. He is known for his unique and innovative approach to street art, using techniques such as chiseling, drilling, and explosives to create intricate and textured murals on urban walls. Vhils' murals are characterized by their raw and gritty aesthetic, which often explores themes of urbanization, identity, and decay, making a powerful impact on the viewers.

Paul Henry was an Irish painter known for his contributions to the art world. He is known for his landscapes that often depict the rugged beauty of the Irish countryside, capturing the unique light, atmosphere, and natural beauty of the region. Henry's paintings are characterized by their rich and atmospheric colors, loose brushwork, and a sense of tranquility and serenity.

Dan Witz is an American painter known for his contributions to the art of painting. He is known for his hyper realistic paintings that often depict urban scenes, cityscapes, and people in everyday life with astonishing attention to detail. Witz's paintings are characterized by their meticulous technique, use of light and shadow, and a sense of gritty realism that captures the essence of contemporary urban life.

Dora Carrington was a British painter known for her contributions to the Bloomsbury Group, a circle of influential writers, artists, and intellectuals. She is known for her vibrant and expressive paintings that often depict landscapes, portraits, and still lifes with a distinctive modernist style. Carrington's artworks are characterized by their bold use of color, dynamic compositions, and a sense of emotional depth and introspection.

Peter Max is a German American artist known for his contributions to graphic art and batik. He is known for his colorful and psychedelic artworks that often feature bold and abstract forms, cosmic and spiritual themes, and a sense of joy and exuberance. Max's artworks are characterized by their vibrant colors, intricate patterns, and a unique blend of graphic design and fine art.

Francis Coates Jones was an American painter known for his contributions to the art of painting. He is known for his genre paintings that often depict scenes of everyday life, particularly focusing on the lives of women and children in domestic settings. Jones' paintings are characterized by their attention to detail, delicate brushwork, and a sense of warmth and intimacy.

Fernand Toussaint was a Belgian painter known for his contributions to the art world. He is known for his genre paintings that often depict scenes of everyday life, portraits, and interiors with a meticulous technique and attention to detail. Toussaint's paintings are characterized by their naturalistic style, use of light and shadow, and a sense of intimacy and realism.

Albert Joseph Moore was an English painter known for his contributions to symbolism and the art of painting. He is known for his sensual and mythological-themed paintings that often depict graceful and languid figures in dreamy and poetic settings. Moore's paintings are characterized by their ethereal and otherworldly quality, harmonious color schemes, and a sense of beauty and sensuality.

Final Thoughts

In addition to providing a comprehensive list of artists and art styles, "Art Prompts: In the Style of 500 Artists" encourages readers to mix and match these styles, and to use them as a starting point to create their own unique artistic expressions. The book aims to inspire artists to push the boundaries of traditional art styles and experiment with their own creative ideas.

By using the prompts in this book as a foundation, artists can explore new possibilities and embark on a journey of artistic self-discovery. The book encourages readers to blend different art styles, incorporate their own personal experiences and perspectives, and experiment with various mediums and techniques. It's a reminder that art is a form of self-expression, and artists have the freedom to create something entirely unique by combining different influences and injecting their own creative voice.

"Art Prompts: In the Style of 500 Artists" serves as a catalyst for artists to break free from the constraints of traditional art styles and unleash their imagination to create their own signature style. It inspires artists to be bold, take risks, and embrace their individuality. The book fosters a mindset of experimentation, playfulness, and creativity, empowering artists to push their artistic boundaries and unlock their full artistic potential.

So, whether you're a seasoned artist or just starting out on your creative journey, "Art Prompts: In the Style of 500 Artists" is not only a valuable source of inspiration, but also an invitation to embrace your own unique artistic style. It's a reminder that every artist has the power to create something truly extraordinary by blending different styles, adding their own personal touch, and letting their creativity soar. With this book as your guide, you have the tools to embark on an exciting artistic adventure and create your own masterpiece that reflects your individuality as an artist.

Don't miss out!

Visit the website below and you can sign up to receive emails whenever Michael Ferguson publishes a new book. There's no charge and no obligation.

https://books2read.com/r/B-A-CKNW-YJAIC

BOOKS 2 READ

Connecting independent readers to independent writers.

Did you love *Artistic Inspiration - The Top 500 "In The Style Of" Ai Art Prompts*? Then you should read *Prompt Engineering ; The Future Of Language Generation*[1] by Michael Ferguson!

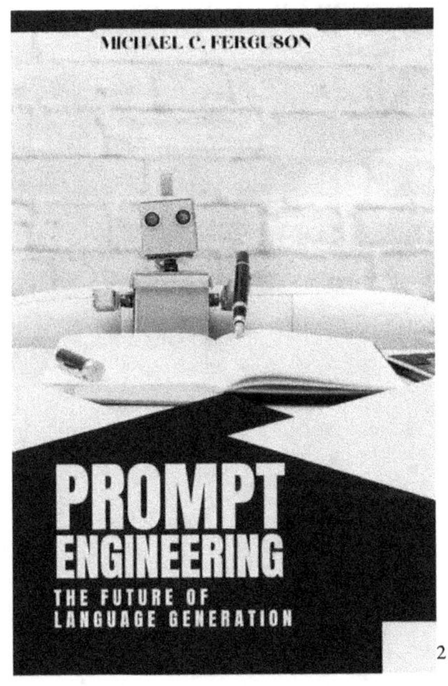

[2]

"AI Prompt Engineering: The Future of Language Generation" is a book that covers the cutting-edge field of AI-powered language generation, from the basics of AI prompt engineering to advanced techniques and best practices for building intelligent chatbots and other conversational systems. Written with the help of experts in the field, the book covers fundamental concepts and technologies such as NLP and ML, techniques and

---

1. https://books2read.com/u/b6VKB6

2. https://books2read.com/u/b6VKB6

tools used in AI-powered language generation systems, practical examples, case studies, ethical and social implications and future possibilities of the field. It's a must-read for anyone interested in the development and application of AI-powered language generation technology, whether developers, researchers or anyone with a passion for technology.